A LEADER'S GUIDE TO SCHOOL RESTRUCTURING

A SPECIAL REPORT OF THE NASSP COMMISSION ON RESTRUCTURING

National Association of Secondary School Principals
1904 Association Drive ◆ Reston, Virginia 22091-1537

A LEADER'S GUIDE TO

SCHOOL RESTRUCTURING

A SPECIAL REPORT OF THE
NASSP COMMISSION ON RESTRUCTURING

National Association of Secondary School Principals
1904 Association Drive ◆ Reston, Virginia 22091-1537
(703) 860-0200

NASSP COMMISSION ON RESTRUCTURING

Vincent E. Barra, Lakewood (Ohio) City Schools
Fenwick W. English, University of Kentucky
John M. Jenkins, P.K. Yonge Laboratory School, Gainesville, Florida
Arthur J. Lebowitz, South Mountain High School, Phoenix
Richard J. Olthoff, Minot (North Dakota) High School—Magic City Campus
Dustin A. Peters, Elizabethtown (Pennsylvania) Area High School
Herbert J. Walberg, University of Illinois, Chicago

NASSP STAFF

Paul W. Hersey, Director of Professional Assistance
Laurel Martin Kanthak, Director of Middle Level Education
James W. Keefe, Director of Research
Thomas F. Koerner, Deputy Executive Director

Timothy J. Dyer, Executive Director

This Guide was prepared by James W. Keefe with assistance from John M. Jenkins and Paul W. Hersey.

CONTRIBUTING AUTHORS

William D. Georgiades is dean of the College of Education, University of Houston, and president of the Learning Environments Consortium.
James W. Keefe is NASSP director of research and vice president of the Learning Environments Consortium.
Theodore R. Sizer is professor of education at Brown University, and chairman of the Coalition of Essential Schools.
Fred M. Newmann is professor of curriculum and instruction at the University of Wisconsin-Madison, and director of its Center on Organization and Restructuring of Schools.

Copyright 1992
All Rights Reserved
ISBN 0-88210-257-5

National Association of Secondary School Principals
1904 Association Drive, Reston, Virginia 22091-1537
(703) 860-0200

CONTENTS

LB
2805
.L315
1992

Preface	v
Introduction: How To Use This Guide	vii
1. The Meaning of Restructuring	1
Forces for Change	1
Reconceptualizing Education	2
The Change Process	3
Table 1. Developmental Staging Plan for Restructuring a School	5
2. Extending the Definition	7
NASSP Restructuring Survey	8
Dimensions, Elements, and Implementation Strategies	9
Quality of Learning Experiences and Outcomes	9
Professional Role and Performance of Teachers	10
Collaborative Leadership and Management	11
Redefined and Integrated Curricula	11
Systematic Planning and Measurement of Results	11
Multiple Learning Sites and School Schedules	12
Coordination of Community Resources, Human and Fiscal	12
Equity, Fairness, and Inclusion for All Students	12
Current Implementation Efforts	13
Table 2. What Restructuring School Districts Do	13
3. A Second-Generation Design: The Learning Environments Consortium (LEC)	15
William D. Georgiades, James W. Keefe	
Origins of LEC	15
Administrative Role	16
Personalized Education	17
Figure 1. Model of Personalized Education	18
Teacher Role	18
Program Evaluation	19
Restructuring Implications	19
Process Components	20
Elements Easiest To Achieve	21
Elements Most Difficult To Achieve	21
Elements Possible for Some Schools and Not for Others	21
Selected Outcomes	21
4. A Working Design: The Coalition of Essential Schools and Re:Learning	23
Theodore R. Sizer	
The Essential Schools	23
The Coalition and the Re:Learning Partnership	25
Early Gleanings	26
The Common Principles	28
Future Possibilities	29

5. A Developing Design: A Framework for a Restructured School ... 30
    Fred M. Newmann
    Structural Changes, Organizational Changes, and Big Changes ... 30
    Arenas of Restructuring ... 31
        Student Experiences ... 32
        Professional Life of Teachers ... 32
        Leadership, Management, and Governance ... 33
        Coordination of Community Services ... 33
    Valued Outcomes ... 33
        1. Authentic Student Achievement ... 33
        2. Equity ... 34
        3. Empowerment ... 34
        4. Communities of Learning ... 34
        5. Reflective Dialogue ... 35
        6. Accountability ... 35
    Culture and Restructuring ... 36

6. Managing Systematic Change ... 37
    Approaches to Change ... 37
        Strategy 1: Fix the Parts ... 37
        Strategy 2: Fix the People ... 38
        Strategy 3: Fix the School ... 38
        Strategy 4: Fix the System ... 38
    Obstacles to Change ... 38
    Processes of Change ... 39
    Managing Change ... 41
    CASE-IMS School Improvement Process ... 41
        Step 1: The School Improvement Management Team ... 42
        Step 2: Awareness Raising ... 42
        Step 3: Collecting Baseline Data ... 42
        Step 4: Assessment ... 43
        Step 5: Interpreting the Data ... 43
        Step 6: Priority Setting and Planning ... 44
        Step 7: Task Force Organization and Coordination ... 44
        Step 8: Impact Evaluation and Reassessment ... 44

References ... 47
Appendix A: Typology of Factors in School Improvement ... 51
Appendix B: Outcome-Based Education ... 53
Appendix C: A*chieving Excellence ... 56
Appendix D: Action Plans for NASSP Goal #1 ... 61

PREFACE

This Special Report reflects NASSP's commitment to a major and continuing leadership role in the reconceptualizing and restructuring of American education. The Report offers a comprehensive definition of restructuring developed by the NASSP Commission on Restructuring. The definition is fleshed out in eight dimensions with elements that require significant action and supporting implementation strategies. Three important restructuring examples are given, as well as a practical process for mounting school improvement initiatives.

We extend appreciation to the members of the NASSP Commission on Restructuring, NASSP staff members James Keefe and Paul Hersey who served as facilitators, and William Georgiades, Fred Newmann, and Theodore Sizer who have generously shared their restructuring experiences with us. Our special thanks go out to the many principals and other leaders at the fall 1991 NASSP regional meetings who critiqued this Guide and made helpful suggestions for its improvement.

The time for initiating systematic restructuring is *now*. We call on all NASSP members and other interested educators to join in a common effort to improve our nation's schools. We cannot wait any longer. The future of our children depends on our success.

Timothy J. Dyer
Executive Director, NASSP

INTRODUCTION

How To Use This Guide

Restructuring will necessarily take place school by school. State agencies and school districts may (and should) provide resources and support, but ultimately, *schools* must do the job of restructuring.

This Guide is intended as a resource and road map for restructuring schools. It provides a comprehensive definition of restructuring, three outstanding representative examples, and a systematic process for implementing and managing change.

Following a few simple steps can help to simplify what is inherently a complicated process.

1. Read this Guide carefully, beginning with the extended table of contents, to obtain an overview of the meaning and the process of restructuring.

2. Note the eight dimensions of the restructuring definition (Chapter 2). Successful restructuring involves dealing with all these dimensions, but not all at the same time.

3. Form a School Improvement Management Team (SIMT) to supervise and manage your restructuring efforts. Include representatives of all stakeholder groups (teachers, students, parents, community).

4. Develop a systematic PLAN, not a piecemeal one, not an all-at-one-time plan, but one that is sequential and comprehensive. Piecemeal change picks and chooses. This is a program or bandwagon approach to change. It does *not* work. All-at-once change can be equally unsuccessful. Trying to restructure eight dimensions of a school at the same time is virtually impossible. What is needed is a step-by-step plan (sequential) that encompasses all the elements (comprehensive). Set reasonable timelines for the plan based on your short-term and long-term objectives.

5. Involve all interested staff members. One variation on piecemeal implementation is to start with only a small select group. Those not involved can easily feel excluded and oppose the effort. When all participate, success is more likely, and early success encourages wider participation.

6. Employ the elements and strategies of the restructuring definition as a checklist to identify initial process improvement priorities for consideration by the SIMT. (The questions listed in Chapter 5 under the Arenas of Restructuring can also be used as an initial checklist.) Conduct a needs assessment. Be sure to build on your successes as well as work on your problems.

7. Decide whether to use the NASSP Comprehensive Assessment of School Environments Information Management System (CASE-IMS) or some other validated system (see Appendix C) to support the process of change. Order the system materials and assessment instrumentation in sufficient time to collect the necessary baseline data for your program of planned improvement.

8. Resolve to start right away. The systematic school improvement process in Chapter 6 can serve as your blueprint for change.

CHAPTER 1

THE MEANING OF RESTRUCTURING

The newest and most profound word in the educator's dictionary is "restructuring." Hardly a professional meeting or a monthly journal goes by without some reference to the need for school restructuring. It is a term found in the presidential recommendations for school improvement and in the meeting minutes of interested business leaders throughout the country. The exact meaning given to the term may vary from group to group, but the connotation is clear. Schools must change if the myriad economic and social problems facing our nation are to be addressed appropriately.

At the center of all the demands for change stands the secondary school principal. On one hand, the principal is asked to provide a school setting where all students can achieve the skills to succeed in today's work force and to lead a satisfying life. On the other hand, he or she is advised to share decision making with teachers, parents, and others so that all have ownership of school improvement.

This report was developed as a guide for school leaders faced with the task of restructuring a school. It is a comprehensive look at the notions of restructuring and reform. It is written to provide school leaders with an overview of restructuring so that a school's progress toward reform can be assessed with some objectivity. It should enable a principal to look at what his/her school is already doing and what still needs to be done.

FORCES FOR CHANGE

As one examines the status of secondary schools today, various local, national, and international forces are pressing for change. After two decades of emphasis on back to basics, comparisons of U.S. students with students of other countries in mathematics, science, geography, etc., indicate that our students are still doing poorly. The National Assessment of Educational Progress (NAEP) survey of student achievement in mathematics indicates similar negative results. Recently, NAEP findings showed that a sizable number of U.S. students could not do fundamental mathematics operations, nor were they able to explain mathematical concepts and their applications. Moreover, although the school dropout rate is about 12 percent and declining, about one-third of all Hispanics do not finish high school. One only has to compare the size of many a 9th grade class with the 12th grade class to confirm that many students leave school.

In a technological society, everyone needs an adequate education in order to function. Jobs for non-skilled workers are rapidly disappearing. A recent report (1991) of the Secretary of Labor's Commission on Achieving Necessary Skills (SCANS) identified three basic skill arenas necessary for holding a job in today's world. They are (1) reading, writing, arithmetic, listening, and speaking; (2) creative thinking, decision making, problem solving, and reasoning; and (3) responsibility, self-esteem, sociability, self-management, and integrity. The report cites the school as the primary source for developing each of these skills in students.

Most schools are now structured very much like schools of the past. In high schools, for example, students attend six or seven classes each day, with little or no variation. Instruction is usually group-centered, with students doing all their work within the walls of the school building. Teaching methods and school year length are the same for all students. Even the middle school movement, which has a major goal to challenge students in multi-age teams, has not affected many schools that still have students arrayed in self-contained, subject matter groupings. It is time to examine these traditional approaches carefully to determine if they are truly responsive to a changing society, to a changing world.

We live in an information society where power falls to those with the skills to obtain, evaluate, and generate knowledge. Young people without the necessary skills to be life-long learners are "at risk," and will likely find fewer legitimate ways to satisfy their basic needs for recognition. Students are different today than in the past. They want their humanity acknowledged first. They want others to know who they are before they are asked to work hard. If students are to do quality work today, they must see school as a place where their basic human needs are satisfied on a consistent basis.

A dramatic shift in school-related demographics is also occurring in a number of geographic locations. California, Florida, and Texas have minority populations that will soon be the majority population. This shift is exemplified by the incoming freshman class at the University of California, Berkeley, where Caucasian students will be in the minority for the first time in the school's history. The faculty senate at that institution passed a measure to require all graduates to complete a minimum of one course in multicultural education. Students need to understand the roles and contributions of all citizens and groups to our culture and to the international scene. A broad perspective was never more important.

The traditional role of the school has been the transmission of knowledge. The advent of more sophisticated technology and the exponential growth of knowledge will soon make traditional schooling obsolete. Students today are able to engage new information more rapidly and more authentically through television, laser disks, interactive video, and distance learning. The Persian Gulf War was experienced as it was happening, not as it was reported in the cooler medium of the printed page. All of us remember watching a news team in a Tel Aviv studio put on their gas masks in preparation for a Scud missile attack. The role of the school must change to help students analyze events and see them in these larger, real-world perspectives. Teaching must become more facilitating than didactic.

This is not to say that many good things do not already happen in our schools. During the past decade, hardly an American middle level school has not wrestled with adviser-advisee or core curriculum initiatives. Few high schools have not implemented student at-risk or school climate improvement programs. We should, of course, build on our successes as well as attack our deficiencies. The issue is neither lack of good will nor adequate expertise nor commitment to student success. It more often revolves around lack of support from district leadership, or scarce resources, human and fiscal, or confusion about where to start.

School leadership is still necessary. Strong reasons still exist for the principalship. But the leadership role of the principal must shift from unqualified control of the total enterprise to the exercise of collegial skills in sharing power with others. Historically, the principal was chosen by the faculty because he or she was the best teacher in the school. It is time to build from that basic wisdom to a broader vision where all stakeholders in the school have more responsibility for its operation.

RECONCEPTUALIZING EDUCATION

The first step in confronting the call for restructuring is the need for a comprehensive definition. Reconceptualizing, not restructuring, is the initial challenge. As many definitions of restructuring exist as there are commentators on education's problems. Some of these definitions are highly abstract; others are more concrete. Almost everyone can agree, for example, with a definition that sees restructuring as "a systematic set of changes in school organization and program that contributes to greater student productivity in learning and potential for life success" (Keefe, 1988). The definition is general and includes the most basic concepts: systematic changes in school operation; and focus on student success in school and in life. Similarly, the Michigan Schools of the Future Task Force sponsored by the Michigan Association of Secondary School

Principals has characterized restructuring as "the re-forming of the interrelationships of an organization; a strategy used to analyze and redesign the organization or structure of education in order to achieve improved student outcomes." The basic concepts—redesign and student focus—are still the main thrust.

As definitions become more concrete, however, the framework of the implied restructuring design also becomes more apparent. For example, the Center on Organization and Restructuring of Schools funded by the U.S. Department of Education at the University of Wisconsin-Madison proposes four domains of restructuring. The Center defines restructuring as "changes in the organizational features of schools, to increase the intellectual and social competence of students, that focus on 1) students' experiences in subject matter learning, 2) the professional life of teachers, 3) leadership, management, and governance of schools, and 4) the coordination of community resources to support education." This conceptualization makes it clear that restructuring embraces changes in student, teacher, and school leader roles and in the use of community resources. The Center goes on to identify 38 criteria that make these four domains much more explicit. The framework of the design is evident and can serve as the basis for school level planning and implementation.

The National Association of Secondary School Principals appointed a Commission on Restructuring (June 1991) to develop a concrete conceptualization of school restructuring. The Commission formulated the following comprehensive definition that will serve as the basis for NASSP's restructuring efforts during the next few years.

Restructuring is defined as the reforming of school organizational interrelationships and processes to increase student learning and performance, with a focus on:
1. The quality of learning experiences and outcomes
2. The professional role and performance of teachers
3. Collaborative leadership and management
4. Redefined and integrated curriculum
5. Systematic planning and measurement of results
6. Multiple learning sites and school schedules
7. Coordination of community resources, human and fiscal
8. Equity, fairness, and inclusion for all students.

THE CHANGE PROCESS

Changing a school is not easy. It requires collaboration among all the players in the restructuring process, with support from district and state-level policymakers and systematic articulation among related elementary, middle, and senior high schools. Several assumptions about change are accepted in the following chapters. They include the following:
- Not all principals are prepared to lead systematic school restructuring efforts but all can do so with adequate School Improvement Management Team (SIMT) organization and participation.
- Teachers really want to help students learn and develop successfully.
- Neither top-down mandates nor grass-roots efforts alone suffice to facilitate systematic change; both are necessary in varying degree.
- Superintendents and boards of education must be in tune with the need for restructuring; systematic change cannot occur without support from the district level.
- The school community must be able to accommodate the necessary restructuring efforts; too much community opposition strangles even the best-planned restructuring initiatives.
- The entire district/school improvement team can prepare and implement a systematic plan for school restructuring.

Change is best accomplished in increments based on careful analysis and planning. Using the eight dimensions in the above definition as a guide, a principal might form a School Improvement Management Team that would begin by conducting a needs assessment to determine the degree to which the school is meeting the eight dimensions. Following the needs assessment, a plan could be developed to move the school initially and systematically toward improvement in one or two of the dimensions. The main idea is to move the entire school toward achieving quality in all eight areas over time. Obviously, the more people involved in this process, the greater the ownership. The development of a systematic change plan should include representatives from all the groups affected by the change. Keep in mind that any plan for change must be "doable." It is wise to think in terms of stages of implementation. The point of entry should be based upon individual school circumstances.

Remember that change involves both short and long-term cycles. The short-term cycle (3-5 years) emphasizes awareness, needs assessment, initial planning, and implementation. The long-term cycle (5-10 years) involves systemwide change both in the individual school and across levels of schooling in the district, as well as institutionalization of the changes. Both short and long-term restructuring require strategic planning. Long-term modifications particularly need a set of principles and processes to guide the stages of restructuring and institutionalization. The most important requisite in either short or long-term cycles is a systematic PLAN. (The restructuring examples described below in Chapters 3, 4, and 5 are long-term designs. See Chapter 6 for a more detailed discussion of the change process and school improvement systems.)

The wise principal begins by becoming well-grounded in the current literature of reform—with an emphasis on the research base. The entire school leadership team should review the history of sound innovations at the secondary level. Reading about Helen Parkhurst's Dalton Plan, the Eight-Year Study of the 1930s, and the NASSP Model Schools Project of the early 1970s is a good place to begin. Each of these programs was ahead of its time and can offer valuable guidance to the principal looking for concrete examples of restructuring with implications for the 21st century. Building on the successful practices of the past makes good sense. Avoiding the mistakes of the past is prudent.

The suggestions contained in this monograph combine the best of the past with the best of present research and practice. Chapter 2 offers a comprehensive description of the NASSP restructuring definition in terms of related elements and implementation strategies. Chapters 3, 4, and 5 present three different but compatible designs for reorganizing a middle or high school. Chapter 6 summarizes specific steps that a principal can take in reforming the direction of his/her school. The appendices contain models and documentation to support the change process.

As we consider appropriate change for our schools, let us do so with care and consideration. The stakes are very high. (The future of public secondary education as we know it may well lie in the balance.) A clarion call for change has gone out from Washington to the statehouses and the local school districts of the nation. A window of opportunity is before us. What we choose to do at this juncture will have far-reaching consequences for the quality and success of secondary schooling in our nation.

In reading the following chapters, school leaders may find it helpful to refer to a Developmental Staging Plan for Restructuring a School (English and Hill, 1990). This plan (Table 1) shows the progress from a Custodial to an Effective to a Restructured School in terms of 14 selected factors. Restructuring schools must address all these factors and do so developmentally; that is, a Custodial School cannot change its organization, staffing roles, and curriculum from traditional forms to highly collegial and performance-oriented modes without progressing through intermediate stages. The sample designs in the following chapters all anticipate a Restructured School in the final analysis, but they also envision stages of short-term planning/change and (long-term) commitment and recommitment to the changing concept base and other factors of restructuring.

Table 1. Developmental Staging Plan for Restructuring a School*

Fenwick W. English and John C. Hill

Factor	Custodial School	Effective School	Restructured School
Concept base	Scientific management	Effectiveness research	Theory Z; megatrends; information society
Organization	Triangle table of organization; principal apex; teachers at the base	Core of principal and cabinet related to individual teachers	Principal and teacher cabinet linked to teaching teams linked to learners and their parents; school committee of parents and principal; house or school-within-a-school team structure
Communication	One-way; formal faculty meetings and information sharing; principal to individual teacher or parent	One-way directed; leader-initiated plus requested feedback	Two-way vertical for issues and proposals by team, cabinet, individual, and principal; two-way horizontal for job-alike consultation
Decision making	Principal has legal responsibility for decisions; teachers perceived as unable or unwilling to accept decision responsibility	Principal seeks information and advice in making decisions for the school; keeps everyone informed of decisions	Much collaboration; decisions made at implementation level; principal and teachers have a clear view of (1) decisions to be made alone, (2) decisions that require advice and input, (3) decisions that are corporate
Leadership	Authority leader; one role identified	Persuasive leader who teaches, persuades of personal vision; leadership core identified	Transforming leader who creates leadership in others; many roles of leadership identified among participants
Principal's role	Manager; implements the program efficiently and effectively; style as controller	Instructional leader; expects excellence in teaching, aligned program, and results in achievement; style as controller-problem solver	Entrepreneur; explores new programs, opportunities, recognitions for staff; style as opportunist, supporter-problem solver-cheerleader-controller
Staff selection	Principal or central office interviews and chooses	Screening with research-based selection tools; principal or central office chooses	School committee reviews portfolios; principal reduces pool to acceptable hires, teaching team interviews for working relationship and recommends top choices

* Reprinted from *Restructuring: The Principal and Curriculum Change,* NASSP, 1990, pp. 13-15.

Developmental Staging Plan for Restructuring a School (cont.)

Factor	Custodial School	Effective School	Restructured School
Supervision of instruction	Evaluative supervision based on board policy	Clinical supervision and technical development to produce achievement results	Peer observation and consultation; mentoring of new teachers
Teaching	Teaching is telling	Teaching is effective telling; large group and intervention for mastery; technical skill in communication and concept development	Teaching is flexible role of telling, showing, guiding, grouping, intervening, and coaching
Curriculum	Discipline-based; separate fields; textbook-oriented	Objectives-based; separate fields; linear sequenced with mastery outcomes	Multiple bases of objectives, personal and vocational goals, and inquiry; both separate and broad fields; mastery of skills and problem centered; personal and social relevance
Learner role	Listen, remember, respond, be patient, be on time, stay in school	Listen, be on task, master basics, repeat deficits; demonstrate performance on standardized tests	Have goals, master basics; learn to find, organize, and apply information; inquire, solve problems
Home school	Parents show verbal and voting support for schools	Parents hold high expectations for students on homework and achievement; volunteer and support the instructional program of the school	Parents create a home environment of high verbal, social, and vocational/professional goals; parents are partner members of learner-teacher-parent team; parents participate in school committee to act on policy and issues facing the school
Finance	District budget determined by past needs for personnel and facilities	Budget priorities established by needs assessment and targets of school effectiveness plan	Site-based budget including personnel options such as differentiated staffing; voucher support determined by parent selection; bonuses in wages and budget based on learning and program outcomes
Accountability	Custodial indicators: e.g., quiet classrooms, orderly movement, polite and responsible behavior, clean facilities and efficient use of funds	School effectiveness indicators: e.g., reduced dropouts, high attendance, and improving standardized test scores; several National Merit semi-finalists and scholarships each year	Learner effectiveness indicators: e.g., mastery skills that are criterion-tested, relating skills, inquiry skills; social/community service participation; career and job goals

CHAPTER 2

EXTENDING THE DEFINITION

Participants at the 1991 NASSP Convention in Orlando, Fla., were asked to consider the question, "What are the critical elements of school restructuring?" Several groups were formed to discuss the concept of restructuring in relation to various factors of school improvement (see Appendix A for a topology of the factors), and the problems inherent in the task. Most participants had positive feelings about restructuring despite the diversity and perceived confusion of existing restructuring efforts. Considerable consensus existed on the need for different approaches based on the varying needs of schools. Great disagreement arose as to what *common efforts* should be made across the nation to solve "school problems." Some felt that schools should refocus on education as the main agenda and stop trying to become a "cure all" for society's problems. Others felt that an even greater effort should be made to address students' needs in all dimensions. The latter would have schools integrate social services into their programs in more effective ways. This effort, it was agreed, would take massive restructuring of social services and a tremendous commitment to the reallocation of resources.

Individual and organizational vested interests were seen as roadblocks to restructuring. The movement of principals, and retirements in particular, were seen as barriers to long-term restructuring.

A number of concepts were recommended by participants as important elements of restructuring. The following were among the most interesting:

- ◆ Provide students with continuous curriculum contact in important subjects to maintain levels of learning.
- ◆ Institute continuous progress learning.
- ◆ Pay attention to higher order skills.
- ◆ Redefine courses and credits in modern terms.
- ◆ Support greater minority participation in society by providing better basic education.
- ◆ Establish site-based management for more effective planning and implementation.
- ◆ Use outcomes-based education to focus restructuring efforts.
- ◆ Adopt the effective teaching model and supportive role of "principal as coach."
- ◆ Articulate whatever is done on a K–12 basis.
- ◆ Focus on skill proficiency, not hours spent or units earned.
- ◆ Establish a longer school year, flexible school day, and more flexible employee contracts.
- ◆ Institutionalize student learning style diagnosis and flexible teaching.
- ◆ Encourage risk takers.
- ◆ Do more cross teaching, subject teaming, and interdisciplinary teaming.
- ◆ Improve teacher and principal selection with techniques like the NASSP Assessment Center.
- ◆ Train more creative, caring, and hard-working teachers and administrators.
- ◆ Develop a proper climate for change.
- ◆ Summarize the valid research on effective teaching and learning. (A new wonderful approach appears weekly!)

- Make a strong effort to understand students' social environments.
- Identify what is really important to teach and concentrate on these skills.
- Prepare some kind of IEP for all students.
- Work hard on elementary and middle level schooling as preparation for high school.
- Teach administrators conflict management.
- Promote shared decision making.
- Consider block scheduling alternatives.
- Institute regular and substantive staff development for all.
- Work at integrating technology—computers, television, interactive video—into instruction.
- Involve parents and community members meaningfully in the life of the school.

NASSP RESTRUCTURING SURVEY

Comments such as those above were used to formulate an NASSP Quick Survey on School Restructuring. A national random sample of 672 middle level and high school administrators was asked to respond to a 12-point survey on selected elements of school reorganization to support improved student learning. Two hundred twenty-five usable returns were received, for a response rate of exactly one-third. Only 7 respondents said that they did not support the restructuring movement. (Perhaps the number is considerably higher. The modest return rate might indicate a sizable lack of interest.) Smaller schools were over-represented in the sample. In every other way, the sample was typical.

Principals were asked to express agreement or disagreement with the following questions. (All numbers are expressed in percentages.)

AGREE/STRONGLY AGREE	NEUTRAL	DISAGREE/STRONGLY DISAGREE

A. My school has building-level control of budget, program, personnel, and decision making.
   67   7   25

B. My school uses participatory decision-making strategies that involve a team of school leaders.
   81   8   10

C. We regularly monitor student, teacher, and parent perceptions of our school climate.
   73   15   12

D. We work hard to incorporate the research on school and classroom effectiveness into our program.
   85   9   6

E. We use a personalized/diagnostic-prescriptive approach to student learning and instruction.
   36   31   32

F. We use a flexible approach to scheduling student time (block, continuous progress, etc.)
   40   18   43

G. Our program makes it possible for the weakest students to learn and improve if they try.
   87   7   6

H. My school systematically collects data to support school budgeting, planning, and program improvement.
   68   13   19

I. My school systematically works with parents to assist them in helping their children learn more successfully.
79   17   4

J. My school believes that systematic school change is desirable and workable during this decade.
92   8   less than 1

K. I consider myself to be an initiator of new ideas and the school change agent.
95   4   less than 1

Respondents affirmed overwhelmingly that they used participatory decision-making strategies, incorporated research in the program, made it possible for the weakest students to succeed, worked with parents to help students, believed that systematic change was desirable and workable, and that they were initiators of new ideas and school change agents. They reported somewhat less implementation of building-level control of resources and decision making, regular monitoring of school climate, and systematic collection of data. They were ambivalent about the use of personalized education and flexible scheduling. To a final question about whether they had already implemented major structural changes, 27 schools (12 percent) responded by providing their names and addresses.

The Convention small groups, Quick Survey data, and additional consultations with NASSP national standing committee members and NASSP Assessment Center state directors underscored the widespread commitment to restructuring. Many schools have already made significant organizational modifications. School leaders clearly support restructuring and believe that its goals are attainable within this decade. They have yet to confront the need for the personalized instruction and the more flexible forms of scheduling that will make this possible.

DIMENSIONS, ELEMENTS, AND IMPLEMENTATION STRATEGIES

The most important task of the NASSP Restructuring Commission was to develop descriptive elements and practical implementation strategies for each of the eight dimensions of its restructuring definition. School leaders in large measure are committed to restructuring. Many are already making important organizational changes in their schools. A comprehensive road map for restructuring was needed. Commission members spent three days developing the following elements and specific implementation strategies of restructuring. They are intended, not as a formal model, but as an outline for the planning, organization, and evaluation of restructuring initiatives.

1. QUALITY OF LEARNING EXPERIENCES AND OUTCOMES

    ◆ The school formally acknowledges the values it embraces. (Vision statement; goals and objectives; supportive school culture)
    ◆ The school community believes that all students can be successful in school. (Vision statement; goals and objectives; supportive school culture)
    ◆ Students, staff, and community hold high expectations for student learning and success. (Vision statement; goals and objectives; supportive school culture)
    ◆ The school positively shapes the conditions under which students learn in the school. (Nurturing learning environment)
    ◆ Student competence is the primary objective of all school activities. (Mastery learning; outcomes-based education; cocurricular program)
    ◆ Student motivation and engagement are the initial focus of all instructional activity. (Relevant learning activities and teaching methods)

- Student learning characteristics are formally diagnosed. (Developmental readiness; subject matter skills; learning styles)
- Students are known well and advised by at least one adult in the school. (Teacher adviser program; adviser-advisee conferences)
- A variety of learning environments are provided for all students. (Large group, small group, independent study, community-based, etc.)
- Students receive specific and timely feedback on how well they are doing. (Advisement; mastery learning)
- Cooperative and competitive strategies are used with all students. (Cooperative learning; projects and contests)
- Cognitive and affective interventions are used with all students. (Remediation and retraining programs)
- Enrichment opportunities are available for all students. (School-based and community-based developmental activities)
- Learner outcomes are measurable and attainable; learning time varies. (Outcomes-based education; personalized education; mastery learning)
- Student achievement is assessed in terms of individual growth. (Systematic formative and summative evaluation; performance-oriented student progress reporting)
- Various samples of student work are used to evaluate performance. (Portfolios, exhibitions, demonstrations)

2. PROFESSIONAL ROLE AND PERFORMANCE OF TEACHERS

- Teacher culture is supportive and collegial. (Collaborative planning; teaming; peer feedback)
- Peer supervision and mentoring relationships are available for all teachers (Professional feedback; role modeling by administrators and teachers)
- Teacher role differentiation is based on individual's skills, interests, and level of responsibility. (Staff differentiation; teaming)
- Teachers have ownership of school improvement. (Consensus decision making and collaborative projects)
- Teachers participate in curriculum development and implementation. (Collaborative planning, design, field testing, etc)
- Teachers base instructional decisions on the best of contemporary educational research and practice. (Teacher professional reading and data gathering; teacher observation and visits to other schools)
- Teachers model and promote life-long learning. (Individual development program; role modeling)
- Teachers are involved in self-renewal efforts. (Individual development profile and program)
- Teachers set and achieve goals for professional growth. (Individual development program)
- Clinical and self-appraisal efforts are individualized. (Individual development program).
- Systematic staff development is provided. (Schoolwide inservice training)
- Teachers have high expectations for self and students. (Supportive school culture)
- Teachers serve as coaches or facilitators of student learning. (Flexible teaching styles and a range of instructional methods)
- Teachers use a variety of instructional strategies based on student needs. (Flexible teaching styles and a range of instructional methods)
- Teachers use technology for instructional improvement. (Technological literacy and skills)
- Teachers teach for basic cognitive and higher order thinking skills. (Cognitive style diagnosis; emphasis on thoughtful classroom discourse)
- Teachers use different kinds of instructional materials based on learner needs. (Range of appropri-

ate print and audiovisual materials)
- Teachers use a variety of techniques to appraise student performance and growth. (Testing, portfolios, exhibitions, etc.)
- Teachers talk regularly with students and their parents about what is working. (Advisement; parent conferencing)

3. COLLABORATIVE LEADERSHIP AND MANAGEMENT
   - Varying staff skills, knowledge, and perspectives are valued and utilized. (Staff hiring and assignments reflect complementary skills, attitudes, and experiences)
   - Team building shows a commitment to staff diversity. (Hiring and assignments reflect gender, ethnic, and cultural strengths)
   - Administrators and staff work together to provide leadership. (Teaming; delegating; shared decision making)
   - Good group dynamics and modern management techniques are employed by the leadership team. (Shared decision making; conflict resolution; listening skills, etc.)
   - Innovative problem solving is encouraged and recognized. (Risk taking; holistic approaches)
   - The leadership team is politically skilled and sensitive. (Communicating and interpreting skills; knowledge of district governance; public relations)
   - An effective communication process is used to promote the school's objectives. (School-site management; group process; networking)
   - Principals model instructional knowledge, skills, and abilities. (Instructional leadership)

4. REDEFINED AND INTEGRATED CURRICULA
   - The curriculum is responsive to local, national, and global needs. (Needs assessment; national goals; recognition of global interdependence)
   - The curriculum is learner-centered rather than subject-centered. (Personalized education)
   - Essential learnings are identified. (Core curriculum; "less is more")
   - The curriculum is internally consistent, and meets legal requirements. (Curriculum mapping and alignment; concern for federal, state, and local regulations)
   - The curriculum contains planned sequences and repetition; no accidental duplication. (Curriculum articulation)
   - The curriculum includes global, multicultural, cross-cultural, and interdisciplinary perspectives. (Recognition of cultural diversity and global interdependence; integrated fields of knowledge)
   - Both knowledge and application are planned products of the curriculum. (General education objectives; skills training)
   - All electives are related to the planned curriculum. (Curriculum mapping, alignment, and articulation)
   - The cocurriculum is aligned with the school's goals and objectives and enhances the curriculum. (Curriculum mapping, alignment, and articulation)

5. SYSTEMATIC PLANNING AND MEASUREMENT OF RESULTS
   - Planning and improvement are based on program evaluation and assessment of student outcomes. (Outcomes-based education; systematic program interventions)
   - Goals and objectives are connected to the school vision and to outcomes evaluation in a continuously renewing process. (Program evaluation and personnel assessment)
   - A long-range plan exists with opportunities for individual input and adjustment. (Vision statement; belief statements; goals and objectives; needs assessment; planned interventions)

- Planning is tied to future-trends data and is proactive rather than reactive. (Data-based planning and decision making)
- Strategic planning, "quality teaming," and creative approaches to problem solving are utilized. (Short and long-term planning; vertical teams; risk taking and initiating)
- Task forces/outside resources enhance school planning and improvement. (School improvement projects; community/corporate partnerships)
- Cognitive, affective, and behavioral criteria and outcome measures are utilized. (Range of measured outcomes)
- A systematic data base (baseline data) is established as the basis for school planning and decision making. (Outcome-Based Education; McREL's A⁺chieving Excellence; NASSP's CASE-IMS)
- Data are updated regularly as the basis for program evaluation and revision. (Formative and summative evaluation; benchmarking; impact evaluation, etc.)

6. MULTIPLE LEARNING SITES AND SCHOOL SCHEDULES

- Multiple learning sites are utilized and connected by design and technology. (Flexible learning environments; community-based learning; communications technology)
- The nature of the planned learning experience is the key to learning-site selection. (Student experiences in various environments—school, community, home)
- School schedules are tailored to the type of learning experience. (Flexible and adaptable scheduling)
- School schedules allow for variation in learning group and size. (Flexible and adaptable scheduling)
- Programmatic options for students extend beyond the traditional day and year. (Extended school day and year; adaptive curriculum)

7. COORDINATION OF COMMUNITY RESOURCES, HUMAN AND FISCAL

- Community and school personnel meet regularly to identify and coordinate services for students and their families. (School-community councils; local school councils)
- Schools and community-based organizations/agencies collaborate to provide extended-day opportunities for students. (Community as school; school-community councils)
- Parents and schools act as partners in the educational process. (Advisement; local school councils)
- Business and school partnerships support and extend learning opportunities for students. (School-business partnerships)
- School district and state funding agencies provide "seed money" for initial restructuring implementation. (Building modifications; planning resources; time for staff inservice and development)
- Community and foundation resources are sought and utilized to enhance student learning opportunities. (Broad-based school financing)

8. EQUITY, FAIRNESS, AND INCLUSION FOR ALL STUDENTS

- All students have access to all curricula and programs. (Flexible scheduling, tracking and grouping practices)
- Program/learner needs determine sequence and flow of resources. (Student skills and style diagnosis; compensatory/augmentation activities for training and remediation)
- Varying learning styles are recognized and utilized in determining access to resources. (Learning style diagnosis and style-based prescription)
- Budgets have student learning needs and differences as the primary focus. (School-based budgeting; flexible budgets)

- Learners with severe disabilities are provided with the least restrictive learning environment possible. (Learning style diagnosis; adaptive education)
- Unfair practices including any that discriminate by race and gender are eliminated from the school. (Vision statement; goals and objectives; curriculum and instruction policies; tracking and grouping practices)

CURRENT IMPLEMENTATION EFFORTS

The elements and strategies of restructuring are detailed under the foregoing dimensions. The plan is comprehensive and systematic. The challenge will require a collaborative effort on the part of school leaders, school staff members, and the parents and communities of our nation.

But is the challenge achievable? Can the nation's schools make such sweeping changes? Is school restructuring really possible in real schools?

Real restructuring can only take place school by school. Each school must confront the decisions of restructuring and *develop a local plan*. But support must exist from the top, especially from the superintendent and school board. Many school districts have already supported restructuring initiatives. Three representative district restructuring efforts are reported in *Restructuring Schools: The Next Generation of Education Reform* (Elmore et al., 1990). Table 2 summarizes the actions of the Dade County Public Schools (Miami, Fla.), the Jefferson County Public Schools (Louisville, Ky.), and the Poway Unified School District (Poway, Calif.). District office and school-site visits affirmed that these pioneering jurisdictions differ greatly in the actions they take first, but all provide leadership, create new organizational structures, and provide support and assistance (Table 2).

The first order of business for schools planning to restructure is to obtain building staff approval and collaboration. The second order of business is to secure district support. School restructuring teams should carefully study Table 2 to determine whether their districts will support substantial change initiatives. If not, the principal and SIMT representatives should meet with district officials (and the school board, if needed) to secure the necessary backing.

Table 2. What Restructuring School Districts Do *

Provide Leadership

Make long-term commitment to comprehensive change:
- Guided by goals, not prescriptions
- Characterized by many reinforcing strategies and steps

Communicate goals, guiding images, and information:
- Create a language for change and a focus on student learning
- Have direct communication between schools and district leaders

Encourage experimentation and risk taking:
- Begin with schools that volunteer
- Support experimentation with waivers from constraining rules

Demonstrate and promote shared decision making:
- Involve all staff in developing educational goals and values
- Limit faculty meetings to items that require immediate action

Create New Organizational Structures

Participate actively in building new alliances:
- Make cooperative agreements with teachers' unions
- Create new joint ventures with foundations, advocacy groups, businesses, and universities

Devolve authority to schools and to teachers:
- Give schools authority over staffing and materials budgets
- Provide incentives for principals to involve teachers in school-site decisions

Promote creation of new roles, for example:
- Teachers as leaders, evaluators, curriculum developers, and facilitators of student learning
- Administrators as facilitators of teachers and as instructional leaders

Develop and demonstrate during the summer new models of:
- Restructured programs for staff and students
- Support for teachers to develop curriculum and educational materials

Create new forms of accountability that:
- Match the comprehensive nature and time line of restructuring
- Use many measures, including those defined by schools

Provide Support and Assistance

Provide a broad range of opportunities for professional development such as:
- On and off-site assistance for teachers and administrators
- Development sessions that include techniques in management, clinical supervision, instruction, and content

Provide time for staff to assume new roles and responsibilities:
- Time for planning, working with colleagues, and school decision making
- Released time for professional development activities

Seek supplementary sources of funding and assistance from:
- State and federal governments
- Local businesses, private foundations, and individuals.

* Reprinted with permission from Richard F. Elmore and Associates. *Restructuring Schools: The Next Generation of Educational Reform,* pp. 244-45 (Table 7.2). San Francisco, Calif.: Jossey-Bass, Inc., 1990.

The next three chapters present in greater detail three regional and national examples of existing, comprehensive implementation efforts. Chapter 3 summarizes a second-generation plan, the Learning Environments Consortium design based on the NASSP Model Schools Project of 1969–1974. Chapter 4 reviews the progress of the Coalition of Essential Schools/Re:Learning working design in some 200 schools. Chapter 5 outlines the focus areas and criteria of a developing design at the Center on Organization and Restructuring of Schools. These designs were selected for inclusion because they represent original restructuring research. Two also reflect successful implementation efforts over an extended period of time. They are not the only examples that could have been cited. They are merely representative. (See Appendix B for a summary of Outcome-Based Education.)

CHAPTER 3

A SECOND-GENERATION DESIGN

THE LEARNING ENVIRONMENTS CONSORTIUM (LEC)

William D. Georgiades
James W. Keefe

School restructuring has been a recurring phenomenon of the 20th century. It has been variously labeled new education, progressive education, staff utilization, school innovation, alternative schools, excellence in education, and school reform. Its longest running manifestation was the progressive movement of the late 19th and early 20th centuries that culminated in the democratic schools of John Dewey and the child-centered schools of the 1930s.

Restructuring has been a continuous political and educational goal since the beginnings of public schooling. Only in this decade have much of the previous thought and activity crystallized in a widespread belief that our schools must *really* be changed.

The Learning Environments Consortium has been one of the most enduring contributors in recent decades to this restructuring tradition.

ORIGINS OF LEC

During much of the 20th century, American schools have sought to develop programs geared to the needs of individual students. Curricular and instructional innovations have been launched periodically in one form or another. In the 1920s, the "behavioral objectives" movement gained momentum. In the 1930s, attempts to sequence curricula and to use teacher aides came to the fore. The Eight-Year Study of the 1930s represented a significant national move to revitalize and change secondary schools, but the advent of World War II dulled its impact. Staff utilization studies and subject curriculum revisions of the 1950s led to the Model Schools Project (MSP—1969 to 1974) under the direction of J. Lloyd Trump and William Georgiades (Trump, 1977; Trump and Georgiades, 1978). Funded by the Danforth Foundation and supported by the NASSP, the MSP advanced three reasons for the failure of previous efforts to change schools:

◆ Most innovations were superficial rather than real. Unless teachers and pupils and the school management team actually worked in new ways, progress would not occur.
◆ No school adopted all—or even most—of the proposed innovations in a systematic, total program. Potential gains in one area were nullified by conventional practices in others.
◆ Schools failed to evaluate all aspects of their programs in the light of competency goals and objectives.

The Model Schools Project advocated five basic changes:
1. The principal must be the instructional leader of the school and should devote about three-fourths of his or her working time to the improvement of instruction. (Reallocation of responsibilities within a school supervisory-management team would make this possible.)
2. The instructional staff must be reorganized. Teachers should have the help of aides who, under teacher supervision, would assume certain tasks that consume more than one-third of the teaching day.
3. Teachers need freedom for educational planning. No substantial improvement in learning can occur unless students themselves have more time for directed independent study; i.e., the opportunity to experience a variety of learning activities away from the constant supervision of teachers.
4. The curriculum most offer continuous contact with essential materials in all the basic areas of human knowledge. It should consist of materials from the real world that the student knows as well as those from the more specialized world of the teacher.
5. Even if all the preceding changes were made, none would be particularly effective without better utilization of the "things" of education; e.g., buildings, equipment and supplies, and money.

The MSP developed each facet of the above rationale in elaborate detail. Thirty-six middle level and high schools participated, ranging from small schools in rural locations to large central-city senior high schools. All sections of the United States, plus Germany and Canada were represented.

The 36 secondary schools of the Model Schools Project achieved varying degrees of success. Five of the most successful agreed to further define the model and to pursue its evolution in their own efforts to improve. These 5 formed a collaborative called the Learning Environments Consortium (LEC). LEC was organized not because its member institutions considered themselves superior but because they shared a commitment to the pursuit of better systems of schooling for their clientele. At the termination of the MSP in 1974, these five schools agreed to continue in a mutual dedication to the rationale of the project. These original LEC schools included Bishop Carroll High School in Calgary, Alberta, Canada; Chalmette High School in Chalmette, La.; Highland High School in Bakersfield, Calif.; Mariner High School in Everett, Wash.; and Pius X High School in Downey, Calif. (See Georgiades et al., 1979.)

The Learning Environments Consortium today is a regional self-help network of schools—a voluntary sequel to the MSP. The Consortium is an independent nonprofit corporation with its own officers and board of directors (the principals and superintendents of its member districts/schools). LEC schools are located in the mountain and western regions of the United States and Canada.

The major goal of the Learning Environments Consortium is assisting schools in developing effective personalized instructional programs. The Consortium is committed to diagnostic-prescriptive education, a supervisory management team approach to school administration with the principal as instructional leader, a personalized approach to instruction with the teacher as facilitator and adviser, and systematic evaluation of all program components. LEC does not attempt to impose a rigid model on its member schools. (That doesn't work.) It simply asks them to work toward altered administrator and teacher roles and performance-based instruction and evaluation.

Regular membership is open by application to schools in the western/mountain regions. Participating schools and their districts make a three-year membership commitment. Regular membership fees are paid by all active members.

ADMINISTRATIVE ROLE

Leadership at the building level is a key factor in LEC schools. In most respects, the school is but the reflection of its principal and community. Principals fill a significant role in bringing about school improvement. The principal, more than any other individual, determines the nature and the success of the school program.

National and state educational organizations have increasingly looked to the principal as the chief instrument of change. The Learning Environments Consortium contends that if instruction is to improve, principals must be willing to work with teachers toward that end. The LEC principal recognizes the need to shift the focus from mundane administrative chores to instructional leadership. Primary among the principal's responsibilities, then, are activities directly related to the instructional program rather than mere management of the organization and its buildings.

The principal, in turn, works with a supervisory-management team. In essence, the LEC philosophy of quality education is heavily dependent on the principal and the school leadership team for:
1. Setting and clearly communicating goals and expectations
2. Promoting a positive school climate
3. Directing curriculum planning
4. Supervising and evaluating instruction
5. Supervising and evaluating programs
6. Maximizing available resources
7. Coordinating staff development
8. Ensuring personal and professional staff growth
9. Promoting collegiality among staff.

Leadership plays an important part in program development, implementation, and evaluation. The supervisory-management team approach, a basic element in all LEC schools, acknowledges the importance of school management, but affirms that the principal cannot do it alone.

In one LEC school, for example, a business manager under the direction of the principal assumed primary responsibility for budgets, operations, maintenance, and custodial planning. This supervisory-management arrangement enabled the principal to spend considerably more time in instructional leadership and to chair a major curricular task force. In another LEC school, delegation of routine matters freed the principal to teach a class and model exemplary instructional strategies for teacher observers. In yet another school, the principal developed and taught inservice classes for his teachers on curricular research and methodology.

In LEC schools, the principal's role as a "teacher of teachers" is a reality. The principal is much more directly linked to teachers. The gap between administration and faculty is reduced.

PERSONALIZED EDUCATION

A significant challenge facing contemporary education remains the critical need to personalize education for all students. Personalized education begins with the learner and builds the learning environment on learner needs and interests as well as societal demands. At the building level, curriculum and program design is the collaborative responsibility of administration and staff. The program paradigm utilized by the Learning Environments Consortium is one of diagnosis, prescription, instruction, and evaluation. The Consortium advocates this DPIE approach because research and practice show its high correlation with student achievement. The Personalized Education model in Figure 1 was specifically formulated in the mid 1970s to flesh out the DPIE model for LEC schools (Keefe, 1989).

Diagnosis is the foundation of a personalized approach. Teachers are personally concerned about student characteristics, learning strengths and weaknesses, and the nature of the learning environment. They diagnose the current readiness, learning styles, and cognitive/affective skills of each student.

Prescription is concerned with goal-setting, program planning and placement, and student advisement. Teachers act as advisers to a small group of students and serve as their primary in-school contacts. They determine appropriate instructional objectives and activities for each student within the context of school/district curricular goals.

Instruction in LEC schools embraces flexible teaching styles, teaching methodologies, and time use, and emphasizes study and thinking skills training. Teachers are involved in structuring the learning environ-

Figure 1. Model of Personalized Education*

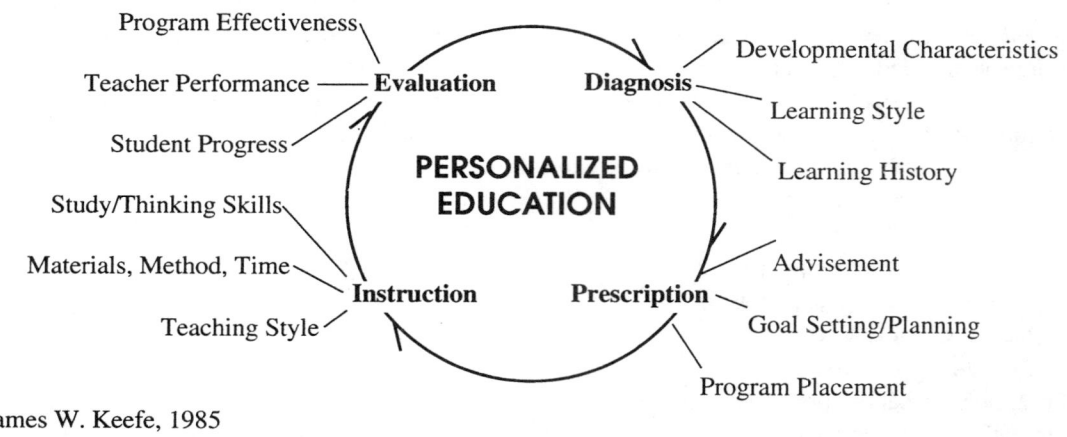

*James W. Keefe, 1985

ment, communicating and reinforcing, monitoring student achievement, and encouraging students in the appropriate use of time and skills.

Evaluation encompasses the processes of student progress reporting, teacher supervision, and program evaluation. It is concerned primarily with student performance and success. It is both the culmination and a new beginning of the personalized cycle in LEC schools. It provides impetus for program revision and new initiatives.

The specific implementation of curriculum based on this model ranges in LEC member schools from a complete continuous progress curriculum in one high school to applications of the "schools-within-a-school" concept. Curriculum offerings are personalized to meet the specific needs of learners. These needs are identified by profiling a student's learning style, learning history, academic performance, and career aspirations. A variety of instructional strategies assist students in establishing competence in basic cognitive skills and higher order thinking skills.

TEACHER ROLE

Personalized education focuses on the learner. Carroll (1975) called it "an attempt to achieve a balance between the characteristics of the learner and the learning environment." Personalized education aims not only at minimal competence but also at excellence for all students.

A key element in school-based learning is the personal interaction between teacher and student. This relationship becomes more productive when the teacher has a plan or blueprint that identifies those factors important to successful teaching/learning. Such a plan or blueprint is the D.P.I.E. cycle.

In the diagnostic phase of the cycle, the teacher assesses the physical, motivational, and intellectual status of each student in order to plan advisement and instruction. An effective teacher recognizes that different students bring differing entry level skills and learning styles to the learning environment. In LEC schools, instruction is designed in accordance with individual needs and styles.

A student diagnostic profile provides the teacher with the necessary information to set meaningful instructional objectives. Teachers, parents, and the student cooperatively develop both short and long-term goals and plans.

Advisement is a basic tool of the prescriptive phase of personalized education. Advisement focuses on the teacher's relationship with and knowledge of the student as person and learner. LEC schools with teacher adviser programs have enhanced levels of student achievement, positive school climate, fewer discipline problems, and generally greater student and teacher satisfaction.

Teachers in LEC schools use a variety of instructional approaches based on the learning needs of the student. Teachers utilize knowledge of individual students to establish a supportive and productive environment. By teaching a wide range of study, cognitive, and thinking skills, teachers help students to "learn how to learn." Teachers coach and facilitate more than they lecture and manage.

As an evaluator, the teacher assesses student progress and provides feedback to both students and parents. The assessment and feedback process has been enhanced in recent years through the use of computerized record keeping. Teachers set high standards and expect that students will meet them. The focus of student evaluation is individual growth, not group averages. Through continuous monitoring, teachers assist students in achieving performance objectives and update the curriculum based on LEC and other evaluative criteria. These criteria are practical guideposts to ensure that learner needs are personalized.

PROGRAM EVALUATION

One of the major reasons for the lack of perceived success of many educational programs is their failure to document student performance. Programs that have emphasized problem-solving skills, thinking abilities, and improved student attitudes have often failed to tell the public whether student achievement improved. Successful programs must evaluate achievement, behavior, attitudes, self-esteem, and a host of other student outcomes (Georgiades, 1978). In addition, the Learning Environments Consortium believes that an effective school must document:

1. A well-defined philosophy
2. Clear-cut goals and objectives
3. A specific curriculum model
4. A systematic evaluation design
5. Communication channels with students, staff, and public.

Effective evaluation assesses the extent of program implementation and the degree of student success. Formative evaluation tells LEC schools whether the various elements of the program have been implemented. Does the principal serve as an instructional leader and work with a supervisory management team? Does the school employ a personalized diagnostic-prescriptive instructional design? Do teachers use state-of-the-art instructional techniques? Does a teacher-adviser relationship exist? Does evaluation systematically measure administrator growth, teacher performance, student progress, and program success?

Summative evaluation tells LEC schools about student success. The following are typical measures of success in LEC schools:

◆ Achievement test results
◆ Satisfaction and self-esteem scores
◆ Attendance, discipline, and vandalism data
◆ Course enrollment and success rates
◆ Graduate follow-up studies
◆ Program cost-effectiveness information.

Several LEC schools are now installing the NASSP Comprehensive Assessment of School Environments Information Management System (CASE-IMS) to generate a systematic school data base for planning, decision making, and comprehensive evaluation.

RESTRUCTURING IMPLICATIONS

The experiences of schools in the Model Schools Project and the Learning Environments Consortium indicate that the single most influential factor determining the degree of progress or lack of it is the effectiveness of professional leadership and particularly that of the principal. More than half the programs have deteriorated when the principals who started the program and worked with the staff to implement it went on to different positions. Schools have surmounted this transition obstacle only when enlightened district leadership appoints new principals who are knowledgeable and experienced in school change when an implementing principal moves on.

Nevertheless, even with transitions and the other problems of change, some components of the MSP/LEC restructuring design have been easier to achieve and some more difficult. In this final section, we will list some process elements that seemed easiest to accomplish, some that were most difficult, some that were possible for some schools but not all, and a few selected but significant outcomes.

Process Components

Elements Easiest To Achieve

1. *Teacher adviser.* Schools found it easy and productive to have each student assigned to a teacher adviser who worked with the students in selecting a program, changing classes or locales of study, and a host of other matters that professional counselors dealing with 300 or more simply do not have the time to do.
2. *Providing options.* Schools learned how to give some students much responsibility for their own projects and development while scheduling other students into relatively conventional programs in the same school.
3. *Developing materials.* Teachers were very successful in preparing learning packages and other self-directing materials for student use. As their experience increased, teachers became much more sophisticated in this process so that the quality of materials constantly improved.
4. *Providing better spaces in existing buildings.* The schools in the project did all sorts of remodeling to provide better places for independent study, larger areas for motivational presentations to groups of 50 or more, and special small spaces for discussion groups of about 15 students. Corridors were utilized better, supplies were stored more effectively to provide other spaces for students to study and to work in, and temporary buildings were better utilized. Better use of the community took some students away from the schools so that buildings were less crowded.
5. *Making schedules more flexible.* Standard periods were replaced with longer blocks of time or relatively open time with occasional reminders for large groups and small groups. More time was available for independent study.
6. *Increased use of the community as a learning resource.* Practically all the schools were able to allow students more time in the community. The increased amount of time for independent study, more flexible schedules, and the availability of teacher advisers all contributed to more community-based learning.
7. *Program evaluation.* With the aid of a variety of consultants, and the cooperation of regional accrediting associations and state departments of education, the schools utilized more imaginative methods of answering the question, "How good is your school?" Accrediting associations readily released the schools from traditional requirements and accepted the criteria that the schools themselves developed.
8. *Evaluating and reporting pupil progress.* The schools found it advantageous to supplement conventional letter grades with a variety of more informative measures. A number of schools developed completely new report forms for students and parents. These forms provided more meaningful information including student performance data.
9. *The supervisory-management team.* Most schools reorganized their administrative team so that the principal was able to devote up to three-fourths of the time to instructional leadership. Other

persons saw salesmen, arranged athletic schedules, policed the corridor, took care of the physical plant, etc.

Elements Most Difficult To Achieve

1. *Differentiated staffing both for teaching and supervision.* Differentiated staffing, including various types of aides, was intended to provide teachers with essential time to develop program materials, improve evaluation, advise students and perform other highly professional tasks. Unfortunately, as time passed, teacher organizations in many of the schools dropped their support. Reduction in assistants made it most difficult for teachers to accomplish the professional planning required.
2. *Implementing the total model.* The unique characteristic of the MSP/LEC effort is that it has prescribed changes in all aspects of schooling. Every school in the project was able to implement some features of the design. Several made broad progress, but not one school completely implemented all elements. Whether this problem will ever be overcome is uncertain, but we know that it took unusually effective leadership and support of the district administration and the community to make progress toward total restructuring.
3. *Explaining the rationale and practices of the model.* In many cases, schools have not been very successful in explaining the project design to their constituencies. Schools are always favorite targets of persons who are unhappy about their tax bills, crime in the community, and other features that the mass media exploit. Good news is not interesting to many persons; bad news appeals.

    It is difficult and time-consuming to go into the community to answer questions of persons who do not come to parent-teacher or other meetings or read the materials that schools prepare. So, many schools have had difficulty (or lack the time) to explain the rationale adequately.
4. *Replicable research.* Although the Model Schools Project and the Learning Environments Consortium have conducted a number of studies and employed a variety of specialists, the resulting data do not provide "sure" guidelines for further improvements. There are many intangibles in change efforts. While some things are quantifiable, many fall in the qualitative domain. More longitudinal and qualitative research is needed.

Elements Possible for Some Schools and Not for Others

1. *Considerable extension of the learning environment.* Students learn in three places: school, community, and home. All three environments need to be utilized simultaneously, and in more productive ways. Only a few schools have been able to expand to all three.
2. *The continuous progress ideal.* A significant element in the MSP model was that students be allowed to proceed at individual (but reasonable) rates of speed when completing course, graduation, and other requirements. Only a few schools attacked this problem in ways that allowed students to complete programs in shorter or longer periods of time than in conventional schools.

    Continuous progress requires almost complete implementation of the restructuring design. Since only a few schools have attained this level of implementation, only a few have achieved the continuous progress ideal.

Selected Outcomes

1. Early LEC *achievement studies* affirmed that students in five LEC schools were "learning as much" in the acquisition of basic skills and factual data as students in more conventional schools. LEC grade 10–12 student scores on the School and College Ability Test (SCAT) and the Sequential Tests of Educational Progress (STEP) were virtually identical to national norms (Scott, 1975). Similar studies continue to affirm this parity.
2. Students enrolled in four LEC schools evidenced a more internal *locus of control* than students in more conventional comparison schools. "Internals" tend to take responsibility for their own learn-

ing and perform best when granted some autonomy, an MSP/LEC goal (McAtee, 1977).
3. In an *organizational climate comparison* of one LEC and one non-LEC school, the LEC school and its teachers showed more positive attitudes toward counseling, curriculum, and school goals than the traditional school (Key, 1977).

Restructuring is both a commitment and a process. LEC schools know that if either falters, school improvement quickly fades. And no two schools change in precisely the same way. There is no one best model of school improvement. Schools have joined the Learning Environments Consortium for a time, and having achieved their goals, have moved on to other challenges. Current member schools are located in California and Texas, in British Columbia and Alberta. The truly notable thing that can be said about the Consortium after almost 17 years of systematic restructuring efforts is that it is still committed and striving.

CHAPTER 4

A WORKING DESIGN

THE COALITION OF ESSENTIAL SCHOOLS AND RE:LEARNING

Theodore R. Sizer

Unlike some current "restructuring" efforts, the Coalition of Essential Schools does not offer a "model" of a preconceived plan to be implemented by a school. Rather, it offers a set of broad, common-sense, research-based criteria—nine "common principles"—that characterize schools whose primary business is to challenge and support all the young people in their charge to learn to use their minds well (the principles are presented at the end of this chapter). These principles guide the local efforts of teachers, administrators, parents, and community leaders as they substantively rethink and then redesign their school's policies and practices to best meet the needs of its own students. Support for these efforts from district administrators, state education officers, and others from the larger community is facilitated by Re:Learning, a partnership between the Coalition and the Education Commission of the States.

THE ESSENTIAL SCHOOLS

There are now some 100 "Essential" schools, the majority middle and high schools, across the country. No two of these are alike. About a dozen have been at it long enough to show substantial redesign in many areas of the school: pedagogy, curriculum, assessment, scheduling, staffing patterns, budgeting, and so on. In all the schools, there are teachers working with students in new programs designed by the faculty members themselves in the spirit of the principles held in common by all Essential schools.

One visits a sampling of these schools and what does one find?

Bigger schools have been broken into smaller schools, using House systems or similar devices. Such groups of some 80 to 100 youngsters served by four or five faculty members have very substantial autonomy, units in a federation making up the whole high school. Teachers and students work together for three or four years and they know each other well; teachers are able to personalize teaching and learning for each of the students.

The schools' programs have a clear focus for all students, without exception. They have yielded sweeping breadth to serious depth. These programs push hard at the students, not only for them to gain knowledge, but also to become resourceful in its use and to demonstrate regularly the habit of that use. The programs focus on mathematics and science, on history and philosophy, on literature and the other arts (often in combination), on forms of expression not only in English but also in a foreign language. The programs insist that young people explain themselves and their ideas, in writing, orally, and through other media.

One quickly learns that a simplified and focused program does not imply some kind of standardized approach. Indeed, when the formal curriculum is simplified and focused, the responsibilities of teachers can be interconnected and focused, thus ultimately allowing a sharp reduction in the number of students for which each teacher must be responsible. As these "loads" decrease, greater attention to the learning styles and interests of individual students can be attended to. And within what at first blush may appear to be a narrowly focused and traditional program, one finds a rich variety of means, tailored to individual students or groups of students, toward common ends.

The schools are noisier, seemingly less controlled. The timing of breaks in the classes is set by each House; there are no schoolwide bells and thus fewer thundering herds down the hallways at predictable times. As the faculty requires the students constantly to display their work, the voices of kids are more likely to be heard than the voices of teachers. As a substantial portion of the work required is collaborative, conversations among students are frequent and consequential. One finds the school library both larger and busier than one traditionally expects.

The students in the schools move forward on the basis of their performance, on Exhibitions. Thus, one finds only rough age-grading in classes. Further, one finds the objectives in courses more clearly defined: both students and teachers are clear on the scope and standard of the expected Exhibitions before they start their work in the course. One listens to students and hears from them a much clearer sense of what they are doing and why they are doing it and where they are going than one normally finds in a typical high school.

An air of respect pervades each school, respect for individuals—even the youngest and most angular student—respect for property, respect for the professional needs and individuality of the adult staff. While one sees the differences among youngsters carefully attended to, one notices the absence of rigid tracking based on sets of one-shot tests. The school is less about sorting and more about education. There still are winners and losers—the human condition being what it is—but the culture of the school presses all students to be winners, and conditions leading to corrupt self-fulfilling prophesies ("I am in the general program, so I can never take that Advanced Placement course") are sharply reduced. Respect also plays out in the school's collective attitude toward youngsters' families and the neighborhoods from which they come. There is tension in this, and as it is deliberately overt, the tension is often sensed. The faculty and students and parents engage continually and intently to address the racial, ethnic, cultural, and economic differences that young people bring with them into the common school.

In the faculty room, one hears as much or more talk about kids and ideas and teaching as about the personal affairs of individual teacher's families or the local sports team. One will hear complaints—the work is difficult, many of the kids inevitably distracted, the support of the community uneven—but one senses less cynicism and defeatism than one might have expected having visited other, more traditional schools.

The faculty teams for each House have authority there, and the school itself has substantial autonomy within the district. With the delegation of authority has come both the frightening reality of responsibility and also the surge of energy released by having more substantial control over one's teaching than is found in most schools. There is more collegiality, more optimism, more articulated stress, and the differences and strains within the school's adult community and their worries about their kids emerge in the faculty room and are dealt with there. In sum, as one listens to the teachers' voices, one senses the school as a whole, most particularly both the attitude of respect for all involved and a commitment that the youngsters must be provoked and coached and supported and pushed to think on their own and to get in the habit of thinking on their own.

The highly blurred line between teachers and administrators is quickly apparent. The principal is the principal teacher, and the team leaders in each of the Houses, in fact, are principals of small schools. One senses a collective vision and an understood division of labor. At the heart of this vision is an agreement that it is in constant motion, subject to collective discussion, and once again one hears the hard but constructive edges of debate over what the school should stand for, what it should teach, and most of all what kind of youngsters it should claim as its graduates.

Such a coherent community, one realizes, does not emerge overnight; it depends on stable leadership. District policy on the movement of teachers and administrators is skewed toward the creation of faculty communities within each school, with a high priority given to building-level stability.

One listens to the students and recognizes that they are in the habit of explaining what they are studying and why they are studying it, why what they are asked to work hard at makes some sense to them for the future, what their obligations are to themselves as well as to the larger school community. They are strikingly confident—at least in contrast with many at other schools—willing to express themselves and familiar in the request so to speak. They are informed and respectful of information and aware that most important things in life are both complex and demanding of thoughtful scrutiny. Finally, one senses from these young people a caring about themselves, about the community that makes up the school, and of the larger neighborhood in which they rest. These adolescents are still colorful, noisy, often outrageous—sometimes even, to adult eyes, fearsome. But at the heart they are sensitively committed to the values underlying the existence of their school, and even as their 15-ness or 16-ness plays out in the theater which is school, the enduring intellectual values which the school stands for, for all kids, clearly emerge.

Nothing that one finds in Essential schools so described is radical or new. Everything that one finds an experienced educator has seen somewhere. If there is anything new in an Essential school, it is that these practices and the principles that underlie them are found in careful combination, not as alternatives or on the edges of school practice, but interwoven at its core. Essential schools are those working to make these ideas shape the core of their programs.

THE COALITION AND THE RE:LEARNING PARTNERSHIP

The Coalition of Essential Schools was established at Brown University in 1984 by Theodore R. Sizer. Its work was preceded by A Study of High Schools, a large research project launched in 1979 and co-sponsored by the National Association of Secondary School Principals and by the National Association of Independent Schools, to seek to understand better the nature and effectiveness of American secondary schooling. Three books emerged from the Study. *The Shopping Mall High School: Winners and Losers in the Educational Marketplace*, by Arthur G. Powell, Eleanor Farrar, and David K. Cohen, provided an analysis that emerged from the careful observation of 15 high schools during the 1981–82 academic year. *The Last Little Citadel,* by Robert L. Hampel, is a series of essays illuminating the history of American high schools since 1940. *Horace's Compromise: The Dilemma of the American High School,* by Theodore R. Sizer, served as a summary volume and reflected on possible remedies that might emerge from the Study's research. The ideas for the Coalition flowed directly from these books, particularly *Horace's Compromise*.

Those of us joined together in the Coalition believe that there is no one model, no one best school. Good schools must take special account of the particular adults and youngsters within them and are respectful of the communities in which they rest. Accordingly, there are no simple patterns, no lists, no precise outline of what every good school must be like. What good schools have in common, we believe, are shared ideas, commitments about learning and schooling that can be played out in a number of ways, depending on circumstances. These ideas have been encapsulated into a list of Common Principles.

A small number of school people and the schools they represented joined the Coalition during the 1984–85 academic year. Given the complexity of locally interpreting the commonly-held ideas—however commonsensical and traditional most might be—the time for planning was considerable, and it was not until 1986 that the first of these schools in fact had revised programs underway. By the summer of 1988, more than 50 schools had joined the Coalition, and two issues had become increasingly problematic: the number of schools wishing to be involved was rapidly exceeding the ability of the Coalition's small staff properly to respond to them; and as the schools' programs developed, conflicts between what the schools wished to do and what was possible under local and state regulations emerged. In an effort to deal both with the rapidly growing scale and with the need to address the regulatory, administrative, and policy context in which

Essential schools worked, the Coalition allied with the Education Commission of the States in the Re:Learning initiative.

States themselves join Re:Learning, with commitments, signed by both the governor and the chief state school officer, to support and nurture Essential schools as they emerge within their borders and, in a parallel fashion, to engage in a "rethinking" and redesign of the policy context in which those schools must work. Significantly, the subtitle of Re:Learning is "from the schoolhouse to the statehouse." Re:Learning acknowledges both the desirability for schools to vary and the responsibility of those schools to develop programs uniquely responsive to and reflecting the best of the communities in which they reside.

By mid-1991, there were some 200 schools involved at various stages in the Re:Learning effort and, within it, the Coalition of Essential Schools. Seven states have become full members—Arkansas, Colorado, Delaware, Illinois, New Mexico, Pennsylvania, and Rhode Island—and as many more are in various stages of developing plans to join. In addition, in four regions—Northern and Southern California, New York, and New England—and in two large school districts—Broward County, Fla., and Jefferson County, Ky.—networking among Essential schools in the area is facilitated by a local coordinator.

The task of explaining the Coalition's ideas and supporting the work of individual schools has increasingly shifted away from the Coalition's central staff. Coordinators in the RE:Learning states and the regions serve as local networking facilitators and liaisons between the schools and the state's educational system. Experienced faculty members from Essential schools (teachers in the Citibank Faculty program and principals in the Thomson Fellows program—named for NASSP's former executive director Scott Thomson) have been prepared to work intensively with schools as they seek to interpret the Common Principles and plan new programs.

The staff at the Coalition and the Re:Learning staff at the Education Commission of the States now focus their efforts in four main areas: ongoing study of the implications of the nine Common Principles, this research to assist and support the emerging work in the schools and school systems; creation of professional development opportunities specifically designed to support Essential school change; liaison with state and regions; and assessment of the overall effort.

EARLY GLEANINGS *

What have we learned thus far?

We are ever more convinced from the evidence that when high school is broken down to human scale—lessening the anonymity that emerges from the typical shopping mall high school—students perform better. The results within schools serving working-class and lower-income youngsters are particularly dramatic here, with substantially lower dropout rates, higher attendance rates, reduced disciplinary problems, and better academic performance.

We have learned that while the task of designing one's own school on the basis of a set of commonly held ideas is initially more difficult than being handed somebody else's plan to "implement," the local focus of the Coalition's work and the respect of the people at the school level bring powerful energy and authority that previously were often not there.

We have learned that pushing more of the work onto the students—the expression of the principle that the student must be the worker and the teacher must be the coach—is both difficult to do and effective in the long term. It is the only way by which students can learn how to use knowledge—much less get into the habits of its use. Pushing the work onto the students and insisting that they engage takes longer and forces classes to abandon strict schedules. Youngsters grasp things in different ways at different rates at different times, and this common-sense notion undermines the (apparent) orderliness of the typical high school.

---

* See the NASSP *Practitioner,* December 1991, "Taking Stock: How Are Essential Schools Doing?" for a more complete discussion of Essential School performance data.

We are learning that in school redesign, small steps, while easier to take in the beginning, are in the long run riskier than bold steps; incremental changes that do not address the fundamental problems getting in the way of powerful student learning simply put off the day of reckoning. We have learned that what appeared to emerge in similar work in schools as far back as the 1930s still is true: timidity carries with it very substantial risks.

We have learned that even those bold plans that are rooted in both common sense and traditional beliefs of teachers require the strong and vigorous support of principals and senior teachers in the school as well as parents and leaders surrounding the school. We are now used to the paradox of communities within and without schools agreeing that "schools must change" but almost paralyzed in addressing the implications of that conclusion for changed practice. We have learned that the incentives to take action upon the critique are on the whole very weak, that even as people criticize the status quo, they adhere remarkably to it. The symbols and traditions of the existing school—again even if criticized by the community itself—die hard.

We have learned that in many cases the realignment of human resources to allow teachers 80 or fewer pupils to get to know is a major stumbling block. The Coalition is committed to the idea that this shift from what in many schools means 110 to 180 students per teacher at a given time be accomplished without substantial changes in the operating budget, and as a result, the adaptations within many schools must be ambitious. Not all teachers like teaming—almost an essential for changing teachers' student loads—nor are all willing to teach beyond a narrowly defined conception of their field. The sweeping variety of courses offered in many high schools gives way slowly to a faculty's commitment that some things are more important than others in the school. In many schools, this student-load-on-teachers issue is the crucial one: If the school cannot find a way to achieve these targets that is politically tolerable and pedagogically sound, there is relatively little effect for the better on students.

If the student-load issue is one major hurdle, Exhibitions are another. "Diploma by Exhibition" requires that a faculty be clear both on the substance and the standards of the work it expects students to pursue. This substance and these standards must be cast in a way which the students understand and which ultimately are expressed in such ways that the students can show they have mastered the work. This goal-setting and assessment obligation resides in the Essential school; it is not imposed from the outside in the form of somebody else's standardized tests or routines. Many schools find the struggle to define the substance and standards of their work remarkably new and exceedingly difficult. We have found that when faculties break through and get deeply into this process, fundamental issues of the nature of knowledge and the divisions among areas of knowledge arise. For example, the kinds of habits that many Essential schools wish for their students—the ability to take a mass of information, break it down, make sense of it, and then move beyond, finding some useful application of this knowledge—is rarely learned well in sharply defined and encapsulated subjects and particularly not well learned in a string of 47-minute snippets of time. Simply, the traditional six, seven, or eight-period day and independently planned and taught traditional subject matters break down. We have learned that while the breaking-down is painful, the reconstruction can be profoundly liberating. More than a few teachers have said to us, "We will never go back."

We have learned that the Coalition's work is primarily not a "restructuring" effort but, rather, an exercise in "rethinking." However commonsensical, better ideas are difficult to absorb and ultimately to use. For example, many of us unquestioningly accept the notion that the coinage of schooling must be the coinage of time, that the number of minutes a student is exposed to something is the most important thing that should drive the program, that notions such as "two years" of algebra or "four years" of English are the way to divide up the curriculum. When one accepts the reality that kids learn at different rates at different times, time becomes a secondary variable, and one begins to build a school and a program around where the kids are rather than where we would like them to be. We know that getting kids into good habits—intellectual and otherwise— requires giving them "practice time" and the opportunity to work on their own. Many of us are teachers because we like to tell stories, to serve as sources of information. Shifting, but certainly not abandoning, this role to being more of the coach, more of a provoker of new learning in kids rather than a dispenser of learning for them to memorize is extremely difficult. Simply, we have learned that it takes time to become an Essential school, and the time is less that of putting together plans than in sorting out the implications for practice of old and commonsensical ideas about learning and schooling which, however persuasive in theory, do not play out well in many of today's traditional high school settings.

We have learned that Seymour Sarason's critique of 1960s school reform efforts was right, that everything of importance in a school affects everything else of importance; that narrow, piecemeal reform, of whatever power, almost inevitably is crushed by the power of the existing routines. The Coalition's effort to rethink and then to redesign school "all at once," while initially difficult, nonetheless remains more promising than what at first appears a more likely way to proceed, by particular reforms here and there in a school. Many lively high schools that we know well have pockets of powerful and interesting work, but many of these isolated efforts appear over time to have no impact on the basic core of the school and thus on its central human and financial resources. The Coalition does not see itself as an effort to create another wave of alternative schools. Rather, the Coalition is about confronting head-on the schools that we have today in their mainline aspects.

We have learned that wisely redesigned schools frequently rub up against district and state regulation. For such schools to survive and to prosper, a parallel "rethinking" and redesign effort must go forward at all levels of the education system. There must be rugged protection of thoughtful innovation; time allowed sufficient to grant a fair trial, this stretching probably over several years; and a concerted effort to inform and promote public discussion about the principles underlying the changes in practice.

Finally, we have found that work in Essential schools is both hard and extraordinarily invigorating. The principals and teachers who have stayed with it for a number of years have watched students who were at first hostile (they were asked to work harder) ultimately become more effective learners; students who understood why they were in school and what the purpose of each class was; students who picked up the notion that we so respected them that we expected them to do the work, to get into the habit of getting their own answers, to learn to teach themselves. By the late 1980s and early 1990s, there were Essential schools with graduating seniors who had had the first effect of redesigned schools, and the performance of these youngsters—still few in number but encouraging—was strikingly different. As several said at the graduation of the first senior class at Central Park East Secondary School, a brand new middle and high school launched in East Harlem of New York City in 1985, "We did what Americans thought we couldn't do."

THE COMMON PRINCIPLES

1. The school should focus on helping adolescents learn to use their minds well. Schools should not attempt to be "comprehensive" if such a claim is made at the expense of the school's central intellectual purpose.
2. The school's goals should be simple: that each student master a limited number of essential skills and areas of knowledge. While these skills and areas will, to varying degrees, reflect the traditional academic disciplines, the program's design should be shaped by the intellectual and imaginative powers and competencies that students need, rather than necessarily by "subjects" as conventionally defined. The aphorism "Less Is More" should dominate: Curricular decisions should be guided by the aim of thorough student mastery and achievement rather than by an effort merely to cover content.
3. The school's goals should apply to all students, while the means to these goals will vary as those students themselves vary. School practice should be tailor-made to meet the needs of every group or class of adolescents.
4. Teaching and learning should be personalized to the maximum feasible extent. Efforts should be directed toward a goal that no teacher have direct responsibility for more than 80 students. To capitalize on this personalization, decisions about the details of the course of study, the use of students' and teachers' time, and the choice of teaching materials and specific pedagogies must be unreservedly placed in the hands of the principal and staff.

5. The governing practical metaphor of the school should be student-as-worker rather than the more familiar metaphor of teacher-as-deliverer-of-instructional-services. Accordingly, a prominent pedagogy will be coaching, to provoke students to learn how to learn and thus to teach themselves.
6. Students entering secondary school studies are those who can show competence in language and elementary mathematics. Students of traditional high school age but not yet at appropriate levels of competence to enter secondary school studies will be provided intensive remedial work to assist them quickly to meet these standards. The diploma should be awarded upon a successful final demonstration of mastery for graduation—an "Exhibition." This Exhibition by the student of his or her grasp of the central skills and knowledge of the school's program may be jointly administered by the faculty and by higher authorities. As the diploma is awarded when earned, the school's program proceeds with no strict age grading and with no system of "credits earned" by "time spent" in class. The emphasis in on the students' demonstration that they can do important things.
7. The tone of the school should explicitly and self-consciously stress values of unanxious expectation ("I won't threaten you but I expect much of you"), of trust (until abused), and of decency (values of fairness, generosity, and tolerance). Incentives appropriate to the school's particular students and teachers should be emphasized, and parents should be treated as essential collaborators.
8. The principal and teachers should perceive themselves as generalists first (teachers and scholars in general education) and specialists second (experts in but one particular discipline). Staff should expect multiple obligations (teacher-counselor-manager) and a sense of commitment to the entire school.
9. Ultimate administrative and budget targets should include, in addition to total student loads per teacher of 80 or fewer pupils, substantial time for collective planning by teachers, competitive salaries for staff members at an ultimate per-pupil cost not to exceed that at traditional schools by more than 10 percent. To accomplish this, administrative plans may have to show the phased reduction or elimination of some services now provided students in many traditional comprehensive secondary schools.

FUTURE POSSIBILITIES

Serious school reform will require both imaginative rethinking about the nature of growing up and the learning of young people in America and the steady and determined support of teachers, parents, district leaders, and state policymakers. It will take patience: the kinds of changes that are absolutely demanded cannot be "put into place" and then "assessed" 18 months later. We in the Coalition and Re:Learning are talking about and acting upon a sea change in the nature of learning and teaching of American youngsters. As one visits Essential schools and senses the kinds of activities found in many of them, one is both struck by how obvious many of them are and, at the same time and upon reflection, how absent so many of these are from the mainline American public school. Yet the times are in our favor, and with the rapidly growing leadership of principals and teachers and others across the country, schools worthy of a sea change in thinking about schooling can and will emerge.

CHAPTER 5

A DEVELOPING DESIGN

Fred M. Newmann

A FRAMEWORK FOR A RESTRUCTURED SCHOOL*

"Restructuring" has entered the dialogue of educational practitioners, policymakers, and researchers with a burst of power, but also with ambiguity. Restructuring represents a concern for fundamental changes in the way schools are organized, but the precise nature of those changes and the priority given to different new "structures" are in hot dispute. Restructuring joins a lexicon of other memorable slogans in the recent history of educational reform (e.g., back to basics, community control, effective schools, choice, cultural literacy). Much of a slogan's appeal rests in its capacity to capture multiple meanings that draw different constituencies together in an apparently common cause. A slogan galvanizes attention and energy, thus offering new possibilities for action, but its ambiguity runs the risk that energy will be dissipated in scattered, even contradictory, directions. The danger is not in the multiple meanings and approaches, but in the failure to clarify the means and ends of the different approaches. The following framework recognizes the multifaceted nature of school restructuring, and identifies six critical outcomes that can be used to evaluate the worth of new structures. The framework is based primarily on a consideration of organizational changes at the *school,* in contrast to the district or state.

STRUCTURAL CHANGES, ORGANIZATIONAL CHANGES, AND BIG CHANGES

Organizational structures can be defined as the roles, rules, and relationships (legal, political, economic, social) that influence how people work and interact in an organization. Changing a school's governing authority from the principal to a local school council, or having teachers perform functions formerly delegated to guidance counselors, represent structural changes. Other changes in how the organization operates may be significant, but not qualify technically as structural changes under the above definition. For example, a new principal might consult informally much more frequently with faculty members, or the school might reduce the number of elective course offerings. Life within a school might also be significantly affected by other "big" developments such as major changes in student enrollment, adoption of a new curriculum, or the hiring of several new staff members. (These may not be neatly categorized as either structural or organizational changes.)

---

*This chapter appeared earlier in slightly different form in *Issues in Restructuring Schools,* the Fall 1991 Issue, Report No. 1 of the Center on Organization and Restructuring of Schools, University of Wisconsin-Madison.

Since the nature of roles, rules, and relationships in a school can be affected in many ways, we are interested not only in identifying changes in formally defined structures, but also in a broader question: In what ways have schools deliberately made major changes in conventional practices—either in formal structures or in other important characteristics? Restructuring could involve a great variety of changes, but no particular combination or minimum set of changes is necessarily dictated or implied by the concept of school restructuring.

Proposed changes in schooling are rarely defended through explicit theories, and even less frequently supported by solid research. Nevertheless, the implicit rationale for most of the restructuring outlined here rests on two main premises: that it will enhance either the *motivation and commitment* of students and educators to learn and to teach, or their *technical capacity and competence* to do so. These can be considered the "will" and "skill" assumptions behind school restructuring.

ARENAS OF RESTRUCTURING

Restructuring proposals and programs can be differentiated according to the emphasis they give to four arenas of schooling. Major departures from conventional practice have been proposed for the experiences of students, the professional lives of teachers, school governance, management, and leadership, and the coordination of community resources with the school. Specific changes in each of these arenas are listed below under "Criteria for School Restructuring."

1. *Student Experiences.* Compared to schools as we know them, how are students' lives different in restructured schools? Changes in this arena include the organization of curricular, instructional, and assessment activities; methods of grouping students for instruction; systems of rewards and penalties for academic work; discipline procedures; and school-sponsored support for student activities outside instruction.
2. *Professional Life of Teachers.* Many restructuring projects aim at changing the expectations and roles that define teachers' work, including their relations with students, colleagues, administrators, parents; their experiences in professional development activities; and their orientations to the subjects they teach.
3. *School Governance, Management, and Leadership.* A main strand of educational restructuring tries to change the authority and power of various constituencies (e.g., staff, parents, students) involved in school governance; to develop new procedures for making decisions about staff, budget, and curriculum; to create new mechanisms that hold staff and schools accountable; and to sustain a continuous process of organizational change.
4. *Coordination of Community Resources.* Recognizing the powerful influences on students of family, peers, and community social context, restructuring in this arena tries to build a more effective partnership between the school and those community resources that, if coordinated more effectively, could enhance student success. Such efforts involve integration of health and welfare services for students and families; programs of youth employment; incentive and mentoring to pursue higher education; and programs to increase parental support for children and their schools.

School and district plans may, of course, include activities in more than one arena, and some activities may overlap with others, but making distinctions between the arenas helps to highlight differing points of emphasis within the broad territory covered by "restructuring."

Below are 38 criteria across the four arenas that might be used to define a restructured school. Are some arenas and criteria more important than others? Should some minimal number of criteria or specific combination be required to qualify a school as "restructured?" The difficulty of arriving at consensus on this shows that we cannot count on the concept of restructuring alone to resolve the issue.

Since the ultimate purpose of restructuring should be to improve students' experiences in school, our Center sees that arena as critical. Beyond this, we view restructuring not as a single categorical property, but in multiple dimensions, each considered on a continuum. The most restructured schools are those that represent the most extensive implementation of the largest number of criteria distributed across most or all arenas. The least restructured schools are those that represent the least extensive implementation of a smaller number of criteria distributed across only one or a few arenas.

The degree of restructuring at a school, however, is far less important than the ends or qualities that the school promotes. It would be foolish for a school to adopt a restructuring plan that attempted to implement the 38 criteria as if adding separate ingredients to a recipe. The school must first build a foundation—by clarifying the educational goals it seeks, assessing its unique needs, and analyzing how it must change to serve the goals. The following Criteria for School Restructuring will be useful in suggesting departures from conventional practice that could help to address some of the problems.

STUDENT EXPERIENCES

1. Is learning time more equally distributed among whole class instruction, small group work, and individual study, rather than dominated by whole class instruction?
2. Do students spend more of their time in heterogeneous groups?
3. Do learning and assessment tasks emphasize student production rather than reproduction of knowledge?
4. To complete their work, do students usually speak and write in full sentences and continuous sequences rather than in few-word fragments?
5. Do learning tasks aim for depth of understanding rather than broad exposure?
6. Do learning tasks emphasize "multiple intelligences" and multiple cultures?
7. Are academic disciplines integrated in the curriculum?
8. Is time for school learning flexibly organized rather than in periods of standard length?
9. Do students participate in community-based learning?
10. Do students relate to adult mentors, either teachers or persons outside the school, in a long-term programmatic way?
11. Is student work assisted by extensive use of computer technology?
12. Do students serve as and have access to peer tutors?
13. Do students have substantial influence in the planning, conduct, and evaluation of their work?

PROFESSIONAL LIFE OF TEACHERS

1. Do teachers function in differentiated roles such as mentoring of novices, directing curriculum development, and supervision of peers?
2. Do staff members function in extended roles with students that involve advising and mentoring?
3. Do staff members help to design ongoing, on-the-job staff development based on local needs assessment?
4. Do staff members participate in collegial planning, curriculum development, and peer observation-reflection, with time scheduled for this during the school day?
5. Do teachers teach in teams?
6. Do teachers exercise control over curriculum and school policy?
7. Are there specific organizational incentives for teachers to experiment and to develop new programs and curricula that respond more effectively to student diversity?
8. Do teachers work with students in flexible time periods?
9. Do teachers work with students as much in small groups and individual study as in whole class instruction?
10. Do teachers work closely with parents and human service professionals to meet student needs?
11. Do teachers receive financial rewards based on student outcomes or evaluation of teaching performance?

LEADERSHIP, MANAGEMENT, AND GOVERNANCE

1. Does the school exercise control over budget, staffing, and curriculum?
2. Has the school been divided into schools-within-schools, divisions, or houses?
3. Is the school run by a council in which teachers and/or parents have some control over budget, staffing, and curriculum?
4. Does the school receive financial rewards based on student outcomes?
5. Does the school make program decisions based on systematic analysis of student performance data disaggregated by student subgroups (e.g., race, gender, socioeconomic status)?
6. Does the district provide special incentives for the principal to participate in restructuring?
7. Do students enroll in the school by choice rather than residential assignment?

COORDINATION OF COMMUNITY SERVICES

1. Does the school have a systematic program for parent involvement in the academic life of students that goes beyond the normal activities of PTO, parents' night, and attendance at cocurricular events?
2. Does the school have formal mechanisms for coordinating with community agencies, offering services dealing with child care, drug and alcohol abuse, family disruption, homelessness, sexual abuse, teen pregnancy, crime and delinquency, economic welfare assistance, and parental employment and training?
3. Does the school participate in an external mentoring program, such as "I Have a Dream," which follows students for several years?
4. Does the school have formal arrangements with institutions of higher education to assist students to continue their schooling?
5. Does the school have formal arrangements with institutions of higher education to assist with staff development and curriculum design?
6. Does the school offer adult education programs and recreational opportunities for the community at large?

VALUED OUTCOMES

A major research task of the Center on Organization and Restructuring of Schools will be to examine the extent to which school restructuring can promote six valued outcomes or qualities of schooling.

1. *Authentic Student Achievement.* Improved student achievement is widely agreed to be the most important goal of school restructuring. But apparent consensus on this point glosses over pervasive disagreement about what should actually be taught and tested. What kind of academic achievement should be most valued? The controversy takes many forms, but chiefly represents an underlying tension between conventional and authentic achievement. Conventional achievement emphasizes the learning and reproduction of specific definitions, facts, and skills that have been specified by authorities. Masters of conventional achievement are winners of scholarships and quiz shows who have stored in their minds encyclopedic arrays of knowledge and who can retrieve discrete pieces efficiently on demand. Authentic achievement emphasizes using the mind to produce dialog or discourse, new materials, and performances that have personal, aesthetic, and utilitarian value. Exemplars of authentic achievement are investigative journalists, computer designers, sculptors, auto mechanics, custom cabinetmakers, and others who tackle new problems and, through in-depth inquiry, produce new solutions that have value in the world beyond the demonstration of individual proficiency.

To be sure, authentic achievement depends upon knowledge of important definitions, facts, and skills. Familiarity with a wide range of information is important for success in work, civic affairs, and personal life. The problem is that formal education is so dominated by conventional achievement that it stifles student engagement in learning, suppresses critical and creative thinking, and minimizes the application of school learning to life beyond school. The point is not to cultivate one form of achievement to the exclusion of the other. To move toward a more reasonable balance between conventional and authentic achievement, the Center will concentrate primarily on learning how restructuring efforts can enhance the significance of authentic learning in school. Instruction in this direction is likely to stress higher order thinking, in-depth study, and substantive conversation about a subject.

2. *Equity*. To the extent that students' educational opportunities are determined by race, social class, gender, or cultural background, the system violates the democratic principle of equal educational opportunity. The "effective schools" movement began with a clear focus on this issue, as does much of the rhetoric about restructuring urban schools. In most schools, however, vast inequities persist. Even aspects of the restructuring movement (e.g., site-based management, teacher empowerment, choice plans), can exacerbate inequities by neglecting to address the issue directly. Administrators and teachers are profoundly concerned about how to respond more constructively to students of diverse backgrounds, interests, prior knowledge, and styles of learning. Research on learning has dramatized the negative effects of schools' failure to adapt instruction to students' special needs. National reports on the changing demography of the student body are plentiful, but policies for reform have given little attention to organizational mechanisms that might respond equitably to pluralism. By focusing on the experience of students of color, women, those from low-income families, and those with limited English, and by highlighting the consequences of restructuring efforts for equity, the Center will keep this issue visible and identify promising approaches.

3. *Empowerment*. Research on organizational productivity in many contexts (e.g., industry, government, service professions) indicates the need to decentralize decision making. One of the most prominent themes of the restructuring movement is to empower parents, teachers, principals, and students. New decision-making structures raise complex issues in defining both the scope of authority of participants and the processes through which they work. To what extent, for example, should a local school be obligated to fulfill district or statewide curriculum standards? Under what conditions should parents be permitted to override teachers' decisions, or should teachers be able to reject parental preferences? How much control should students have over the planning, execution, and evaluation of their schoolwork? What is the principal's place in all this?

Empowerment of teachers can expand their responsibilities beyond the role of instruction in a self-contained classroom. Broader responsibilities for school curriculum hiring, budget, and interaction with parents present new demands that can actually decrease teachers' opportunities to reflect systematically on instruction. How will new structural arrangements offer teachers, students, and parents the resources (additional time and knowledge) needed to exert influence? How will schools respond to teachers who prefer not to be "empowered"? The Center will examine the ways in which teachers, students, and parents are empowered within schools, and the apparent costs and benefits in terms of the five other outcomes.

4. *Communities of Learning*. Research suggests that society in general, and education in particular, could benefit substantially from efforts to transform impersonal bureaucratic organizations into places where participants share goals and pursue a common agenda through collaborative activities that involve stable, personalized contact over the long term. In communities of learning, all teachers and students feel included as full-fledged participants in the school; teachers and students relate to one another more as whole persons; they participate in and take responsibility for the collective life of the school; and they can count upon one another for help in meeting both individual and collective needs.

Tightly knit communities can, of course, become oppressive and restrict individual choice and expression. In communities of learning, however, members support the right of all students to develop as individuals. This commitment, and an "ethic of caring" based on respect for each individual, protects against the potentially negative qualities.

At least three powerful social forces work against building community in schools. The first is cultural differentiation related to race, ethnicity, class, gender, and urbanicity. The second is professionalization (including specialization of knowledge). The third is the culture's value on individual autonomy as the most important criterion for quality of life. Each of these push toward differentiated rather than common experience and goals, making it increasingly difficult to organize schools into unified communities.

Restructuring initiatives such as cooperative and small group learning, teacher teaming, site-based management, developing a core curriculum for all, schools-within-schools, reducing school size, or magnet schools are consistent with the effort to build a community of learning. But these alone will not necessarily develop community or sustain it. The Center will study how such efforts and others contribute to the building and sustaining of community, the difficulties encountered, and how to overcome them.

5. *Reflective Dialogue.* Research on student learning, teaching, and educational and social change is beginning to converge on a central insight: belief systems **cannot** be changed by a unilateral imposition or simple replacement of an old belief with a new one. Instead, beliefs change through dialogue that stimulates open, nonthreatening questioning, and through the testing of basic assumptions by exposure to new experiences. The failure of the curriculum reform movement of the 1960s can be explained largely by its neglect of this point. Curriculum packages, for example, were sometimes developed in isolation from practicing teachers who were then expected to adopt them simply on the face value. In short, mandates, regulations, and materials are not enough. Unless restructuring efforts support opportunities for dialogue, substantial change in educational practice is unlikely.

Reflective dialogue allows teachers, administrators, policymakers, and parents to make decisions about optimal educational practice after careful study and honest discussion. This requires time, the willingness to probe deeply and to entertain unconventional ideas, and, most important, access to new knowledge and ideas. Without reflective dialogue, educators are likely to implement the kinds of ultimately useless innovations that have plagued schools for years. Without reflective dialogue, even potentially effective innovations are doomed. Unless teachers personally and collectively conclude that a given change ought to be tried, they are unlikely to invest in making it work. The Center will try to learn how various approaches to school restructuring create or suppress opportunities for reflective dialogue about educational practice and change.

6. *Accountability.* At the state and district levels, the accountability theme represents a major shift in thinking about how to enhance educational quality. Rather than attempting to control and regulate the process of education (e.g., course credits, curriculum content, staffing ratios), schools will be held more accountable for student outcomes. Increased accountability is usually not carefully defined, but it usually means gathering more precise information about student achievement on a periodic basis:

- Through indicators that can be compared over time across classrooms, schools, and districts making the information more widely accessible to the public; and
- Allocating more dramatic (positive and negative) consequences for performance to students, teachers, schools, and districts.

Holding schools accountable for student achievement can be a valued outcome in the sense that taxpayers, parents, and students are entitled to good documentation of the quality of service that schools offer. Since many schools have not traditionally supplied meaningful information of this sort (grades and standardized test scores give very little useful information about what the students have learned in school), the press for accountability may be considered a positive step.

At the same time, restructuring for increased school accountability raises several unresolved issues. Little consensus exists on what standards should be used to evaluate student performance. This ambiguity poses serious problems if the point of accountability is to enable the public to compare schools. The specific incentives or sanctions used to motivate students, teachers, and administrators have yet to be clarified. High-stakes accountability systems could conceivably support or undermine each of the other five valued outcomes, depending upon the content and procedures of school assessment. Standardized achievement tests, for example, tend to emphasize conventional forms of student achievement to the neglect of authentic achievement. Some approaches to the reporting of data fail to reveal the disparity in achievement between racial, ethnic, and socioeconomic groups. The Center will study the extent to which schools are held accountable for student performance, but it will be most interested in how accountability mechanisms can support, rather than undermine, the other five valued outcomes.

CULTURE AND RESTRUCTURING

It is important to realize that any single organizational structure (e.g., school-site council, heterogeneous grouping, teacher mentors, longer school day, team teaching) is unlikely alone either to advance or to impair the valued outcomes. It all depends upon how the innovations are employed. The use of organizational innovation is influenced largely by the values, beliefs, and technical capacity that individuals bring to their work. Educators' instructional goals, their knowledge of subject matter, their patterns of interaction, their commitment to excellence, equity, or the development of children, their receptiveness to innovation itself—all these comprise the "content" that ultimately determines what impact schools have on students. We have seen instances, for example, of schools where committed staff members with minimal structural support offer more authentic instruction to students than in other schools where some structural supports (e.g., common planning time for teachers) are superior, but the opportunities are not used.

Since organizational structures may help to facilitate progress toward certain outcomes, but cannot guarantee them, we must pay careful attention to school culture, which often seems to be the most powerful factor in comprehending "everyday life" in schools. Culture affects how structures are used; structures, in turn, provide opportunities, limits, incentives, and sanctions that affect culture. The problem for research is not simply to determine how specific structures alone produce valued outcomes, but how structure and culture interact to do so.

This framework for clarifying the means and ends of school restructuring was developed to guide the Center's five-year program of research. We hope that it will also help teachers, school administrators, and policymakers to understand the issues they confront and to consider new possibilities.

CHAPTER 6

MANAGING SYSTEMATIC CHANGE

Many school leaders are already wary of the "R word." They feel a certain pressure to do something but are not really sure where to start. Even comprehensive examples like LEC and the Essential School's Coalition more overwhelm some practitioners than stimulate them to action. Change is a complex process and is influenced by many forces. Fernandez (Elmore et al., 1990) puts it this way: "Change is scary. Any venture into the unknown is uncomfortable and involves a degree of risk."

During the past 40 years, three major "perspectives" on the change process have emerged from the research literature. House (1981) describes them as follows:

- The rational-scientific or R&D perspective—Give school people valid information on improvements and they will apply them;
- The political perspective—Mandate changes from federal or state levels or give schools permission to change if certain conditions are met; and
- The cultural perspective—Improvements occur only with changes in values and expectations within a district or school. The R&D perspective, typical of the 1950's–1970s proved to be naive. The political perspective, dominant during the 1980s, resulted in (equally naive) top-down reforms that achieved little. The cultural perspective, nurtured by the school climate/culture movement (and also employed widely in the business sector), propels the bottom-up restructuring efforts of the 1990s.

APPROACHES TO CHANGE

None of these perspectives has yet produced long-term, systematic, institutionalized change in schools. The cultural perspective, however, incorporates the best of the R&D and political perspectives, and has great potential for success. Sashkin and Egermeier (1991) propose that the perspectives have resulted in four broad strategies for changing schools. Each of the strategies accepts certain assumptions about why people change and includes various programs and actions to drive change.

The first three strategies represent more traditional approaches to change; the fourth synthesizes the most successful tactics of the earlier three and can serve as a foundation for current restructuring efforts.

- *Strategy 1: Fix the Parts by Transferring Innovations.* Get new information into practice by developing and transferring specific curricular or instructional programs. Make principals effective instructional leaders, make teachers effective instructors, fix math or reading courses. When the innovations include only stand-alone information (the latest fad or program), they are less likely to be implemented or institutionalized. When they provide technical assistance (like the Agricultural Extension Service or "county agent" model in farming), they are more likely to be adopted—or in reality, adapted. The best of the R&D programs, like the U.S. Department of Education's National Diffusion Network, or the "effective schools" movement, can be very successful, particularly if the press for improvement emphasizes change in school culture or climate. The NASSP Assessment and Development network located in approximately 35 states is another example of a successful support system for principals that has been effective in initiating and monitoring innovation in personnel development.

- *Strategy 2: Fix the People by Training and Developing Professionals.* Comprehensive school improvement requires remodeled preservice training of administrators and teachers and systematic administrator/teacher inservice training. Initiatives at the college level such as the Holmes Group's call for reform of teacher training, and school-based programs like Madeline Hunter's Instructional Theory into Practice (also called mastery teaching or Program for Effective Teaching), focus more on staff development than program improvement. They have tended to generate widespread interest and adoption, but ultimately fail to produce real improvement because they remain theoretical or program evaluations are disappointing. Recent work by Fullan (1990) attempts to tie staff development directly to school improvement. Fullan argues that this difficult but workable process requires (once again) changing the wider culture of the school and the classroom. No evaluation data are yet available.

- *Strategy 3: Fix the School by Developing the Organization's Capacities To Solve Problems.* Help people in the school as an organization to solve their own problems more successfully. This strategy grew out of the organization development (OD) movement that has schools collect data to identify and solve problems and to evaluate whether solutions really work. The best of the OD models focus on changing the organization's culture and on long-term improvement with the assistance of trained consultants. One of the most widely implemented—the Northwest Regional Educational Laboratory's Onward to Excellence model—is validated for individual school use and is now being tested for district-level application. These OD approaches have not been generally available and can be expensive to implement. Mid-Continent Regional Educational Laboratory's A⁺chieving Excellence and NASSP's new Comprehensive Assessment of School Environments Information Management System (CASE-IMS) are intended to provide schools with systematic data-gathering, planning, and evaluating capabilities without the need for costly consultants. OD models do work, but "readiness for change" in the form of common goals and skills in communication and collaboration are prerequisites to success.

- *Strategy 4: Fix the System by Comprehensive Restructuring.* Adopt/adapt the best of the innovative program, staff development, and organizational development strategies in a multilevel approach involving individual schools, districts, state agencies, and reaching out to effect cultural change in the community. This strategy represents a synthesis of the wisdom about educational change and school reform. It undergirds such current efforts as the Coalition of Essential School's Re:Learning partnerships in seven states and Maine's Restructuring Schools Program in 10 schools. At the individual school level, it emphasizes widespread linkages of the restructuring unit with state, district, business, and other community agencies. Hence, it is often called *systemic* change. It moves beyond single-dimension strategies to address the problems of the context or the wider environment in which the school must function. It also recognizes that this wider system can produce obstacles to change, even change that is well-conceptualized, funded, and implemented.

OBSTACLES TO CHANGE

Adam Urbanski (1991) of the Rochester Teachers Association writes about the current restructuring experiments in the Rochester City Schools in this way:

> Real change is real hard. It is an inductive process, a search. Along the way we have encountered some false starts, wrong turns, and negative findings. We experienced turf wars . . . , community opposition . . . , and resistance from some teachers. . . . Yet the pain involved may in itself be evidence that the changes we are attempting are substantive.
>
> And real change also takes real time. Expecting extraordinary results very quickly is unrealistic. As Fred Hechinger, the former education writer for the *New York Times,* has pointed out, that would be like planting a young tree and then pulling it up once a week to see how the roots are taking hold.

Various problem themes recur in any program of planned change. Charters and Pellegrin (1973) compiled the following problem list for consideration by schools attempting comprehensive improvements. Obstacles to change include:

- Unclear goals—what you hope to accomplish.
- Assumption that *behavioral* changes will follow structural changes—new structures help but do not cause change.
- Same assumption for *values*—program philosophy must be internalized by staff, students, and parents. Communication and conversation are necessary.
- Same assumption for *objectives*—support structures are needed, such as time for inservice training and development of materials.
- Unrealistic time perspective—5 to 10 years are required for long-term, institutionalized improvements.
- Untrained staff—staff development and deployment are often inadequate.
- Role overload—unclear position descriptions or unrealistic start-up work load to plan/implement the changes.
- Lack of resources—deficiencies in the school building, media, and reference materials, and in community support.
- Lack of evaluation technology—insufficient total program evaluation.
- Inadequate ideology of self-governance—unsatisfactory administrative organization, communication channels, school-based and participatory structures.

Moreover, too much standardization or early incorporation can ruin otherwise successful efforts. Adopting the same procedures throughout the entire school (or district) to offset increased work load or in response to parent or teacher criticisms can result in loss of flexibility and creativity. And, the ever-present temptation to end the implementation effort too soon (after two to three years) in response to emotional exhaustion or loss of key personnel points up the need for long-term planning, perseverance, and staff stability. Walcott (1973) called the period preceding incorporation of an improvement the "intensive half-life" of the innovation. This is the period in which great effort, vast amounts of time, and considerable money are expended in getting started.

PROCESSES OF CHANGE

The biggest challenge to restructuring is "running the existing enterprise at full tilt, while creating and introducing a new one," according to the National LEADership Network's Study Group on Restructuring (1991). Another is what Richard Elmore (*Education Week,* 1988) calls the $64,000 question: How to keep restructuring focused on the central goal of improving teaching and learning. In the same *Education Week* report on "The Restructuring Puzzle," Lee Shulman of Stanford University comments, "For too many people, restructuring has become an end in itself. They've lost sight of the fact that the purpose of restructuring is not empowerment, but enablement. It's not to give teachers more power; it's to give them the ability to respond appropriately to kids. The way to go about this," he proposes, "is first to ask, 'What are the sorts of things that teachers are not doing, or cannot do, that would be good for kids?' And then, 'How would you change the structure to make things possible?'"

Each school must do just that. Start by asking all stakeholders in the school (parents, students, teachers, wider community) just what needs to be done to improve the school. (This is a needs assessment.) Then the professional staff and parents must acquire the skills to provide more personalized learning for students. This implies systematic staff development for teachers and adequate resources for personalization. It also implies time for learning to use these new tools. It requires a PLAN—before, during, and after implementation. It also requires adequate evaluation technology to collect and evaluate the necessary data for planning, decision making, and implementation. Recent Phi Delta Kappa Fastbacks succinctly detail many of these restructuring processes from various perspectives: school redesign (Villars, 1991), school-site restructuring (McCarthy,

1991), urban school restructuring (Weinholz, 1991), and restructuring through technology (Frick, 1991).

The Coalition of Essential Schools (*Horace*, November 1991) reports that a number of conditions must be fostered and linked if new norms for dealing with conflict, risk, or change are to be created. These include:

- Ample paid or released time for reflection or conversation: not just retreats or "day-away" programs, but time built into the teachers' daily schedule.
- A small enough student load so that teachers know their students well, and have the energy to think and talk creatively about their needs.
- Public and positive feedback by the administration for taking risks in the classroom, even if they do not always succeed.
- Regular meetings of the entire faculty to address substantive educational issues over which they have real power.
- Involving virtually every teacher in shaping some aspect of what is at stake.
- Including in the conversations those students, parents, and teachers not in the vanguard of change.

The 15-year experience of the Learning Environments Consortium would add the following elements to the plan.

- Early formation of a supervisory-management team to provide leadership for the change effort. (It may well be a School Improvement Management Team.)
- Concern for collecting good diagnostic data on each student and, in particular, diagnosing each student's cognitive/learning style.
- Helping teachers and others to become advisers or mentors so that every student has a personal advocate and friend in the school.
- Helping teachers to become facilitators of learning (or coaches) rather than just tellers and evaluators.
- Involving teachers in curriculum redesign (Sizer reminds us that "less is more") and in personalizing the learning process for students.
- Providing a school schedule that is flexible enough to support personalized and technology-based approaches to instruction and learning (e.g., block schedules, continuous progress approaches).
- Collecting systematic evaluation data on all significant elements of the change effort, with a particular concern for a variety of student outcomes.

Involving parents and community members in the effort is also critical to success. Coleman (1991) stresses that encouraging parents to *help one another* is fundamental to lasting school improvement. Many parents are estranged from their own children, cut off from other parents, and uninvolved with the school. The principle of "in loco parentis" governing school authority to function reasonably over students' school-day behavior is virtually dead. Schools need parental support and goodwill to operate effectively. Unpleasant contacts between parents and the school are usually the school's fault. "If the school waits for parents to initiate contact," Coleman says, "the contact is likely to be about a problem, and potentially antagonistic. . . . Most parents are occupied with other matters, and will not become actively involved with other parents unless that activity satisfies a particular interest."

Relationships established among parents for a specific purpose (cocurricular activities; crisis interventions) can last over time and build the investment in school and community necessary for successful change.

Existing restructuring efforts can also teach us some important lessons about dealing with obstacles to organizational change. Researchers studying the New York City Schools of Tomorrow . . . Today project observed and reported some important action principles (Lieberman, 1991).

1. Change causes conflict because involving more people unearths new opinions and new problems.
2. Participants in change must learn to trust, which may be difficult for those comfortable with the traditional bureaucracy.
3. Teams must include as many persons as possible to avoid an elitist label or even active resistance from

those excluded.
4. The process of change is as important as the content. Teams must build trust and commitment along with the skills of school improvement.

MANAGING CHANGE

Traditionally, schools have been resistant to comprehensive change because the needed instrumentation and manageable, well-defined processes for school improvement have not been available. That is no longer true.

Today, second-generation technologies such as the Mid-Continent Regional Educational Laboratory's (McREL) A⁺chieving Excellence (Hutchins, Mayeski, and Salley, 1991), and NASSP's Comprehensive Assessment of School Environments Information Management System (CASE-IMS) make strategic analysis, program planning, and comprehensive evaluation possible for any school improvement management team. NASSP has recently released a short monograph describing *The CASE-IMS School Improvement Process* (Howard and Keefe, 1991). This report provides a road map for schools initiating restructuring efforts or desiring to establish a systematic data base to guide such an effort. The CASE-IMS model and improvement process are outlined in the following pages. More information on McREL's A⁺chieving Excellence may be found in Appendix C.

NASSP has sponsored, for the past nine years, a small task force of experts dedicated to creating a comprehensive, computerized, outcomes-based system for improving or restructuring a school.

This system is called the "Comprehensive Assessment of School Environments—Information Management System" (CASE-IMS). The system consists of:

- Instruments for assessing 34 input, mediating, and outcome variables of a school environment
- Computer software for scoring response sheets and for interpreting data
- Procedures for predicting the effect of alternative paths of action on a school's outcomes
- More than 800 suggested interventions for positively affecting selected variables
- A step-by-step process for translating assessment information into significant school improvement projects.

The following section outlines a validated school improvement process using the CASE-IMS system. CASE-IMS is a total school management profiling and planning system. The CASE-IMS software profiles 34 district and school variables, including climate, satisfaction, and six student outcomes. Data from these measures can be compared with validated national standards and cross-group analyses made of student, teacher, and parent perceptions of climate and satisfaction.

CASE-IMS variables are keyed to an extensive bank of school improvement interventions that can aid in local school planning and decision making. A unique program feature permits users to change the value of any alterable variable to ask "what if" questions. For example: What would it take for your school to raise student achievement or satisfaction by 10 percent? The CASE-IMS program can help pose and answer these types of questions.

The CASE-IMS was developed by NASSP's national Task Force on School Environments and has been stringently validated and field tested. The software will support planning and budgeting decisions, board presentations, accreditation reports, etc. In combination with the eight-step school improvement process described in this chapter, it is a state-of-the-art-system for data-based, outcomes-based school improvement.

CASE-IMS SCHOOL IMPROVEMENT PROCESS

The eight-step process outlined below was successfully field tested in four pilot schools and found to be a useful vehicle to translate the CASE-IMS model into action.

Step 1: The School Improvement Management Team

Managing school restructuring or improvement is a long-term, complex, demanding process. The process, however, functions smoothly if tasks are shared by management team members and other leaders. The principal should form a school improvement management team (SIMT). The SIMT is not an advisory group. Its function is to plan, coordinate, and manage the change process. In some schools, an existing leadership group such as the principal's cabinet may be expanded to assume the new responsibilities associated with comprehensive change.

Individuals should be invited to join the management team on the basis of their commitment to school improvement, their proven leadership ability, their willingness to work, and their unique talents. Members may be staff members, students, parents, or community-based leaders. At a later stage (Step 6), task force leaders should join the SIMT.

Prior to the SIMT's first meeting, the principal should prepare a brief "Statement of Purpose" outlining the responsibilities of the team. This list of responsibilities should include:

- Informing parents, staff, and students about the purposes of the process and its intended outcomes (Step 2);
- Collecting baseline data on the CASE-IMS outcome variables (Step 3);
- Conducting the assessment, and reporting and interpreting the data on the 34 CASE-IMS variables (Step 4);
- Performing a "What If" analysis and obtaining from the CASE-IMS suggestions for appropriate restructuring or improvement interventions (Step 5);
- Planning and managing the priority-setting/planning workshop (or workshops) (Step 5);
- Organizing and coordinating the work of three to five school improvement task forces (Steps 6 and 7); and
- Conducting annual evaluations of the school's improvement efforts (Step 8).

Step 2: Awareness Raising

Prior to administering the assessment instruments, the SIMT should sponsor a series of awareness-raising activities. These activities are designed to acquaint staff members, students, parents, and key community leaders with the team's expectations, the rationale of restructuring, and the eight-step process.

Activities might include:

- Staff development sessions designed to enhance staff understanding and involvement in restructuring and the eight-step process;
- Awareness-raising meetings for parents and community leaders;
- Information disseminated through community newspapers, the school newspaper, and special publications;
- Presentations by members of the SIMT to community organizations such as service clubs.

Step 3: Collecting Baseline Data

Data on the six CASE-IMS outcome variables and any other selected outcomes should be collected as the baseline for restructuring efforts. The CASE-IMS outcomes are:

- *Student Satisfaction:* The means of student responses on eight subscales of the NASSP Student Satisfaction Survey;
- *Total Achievement:* Combined student reading comprehension and total math scores;
- *Percentage of Students Receiving Discipline Referrals:* The incidence of behavior problems in the school;
- *Percentage of Students Passing All Courses:* A measure of schoolwide success;

- *Student Self-Efficacy:* The mean of student responses to the Brookover Self-Concept of Ability Scale on the CASE-IMS Student Report Form;
- *Percentage of Students Completing the School Year:* The rate of students not dropping out of school.

These outcomes are collected as a regular part of the CASE-IMS process. These and other data constitute the baseline (and benchmarks) that will enable the SIMT, each year, to measure the impact of the school's restructuring or improvement efforts.

Staff, students, and parents may expect that as the quality of the school environment improves, outcome variables as measured will be positively affected.

Step 4: Assessment

The current CASE-IMS system has seven instruments:

- School Climate Survey (55 items) to obtain the perceptions of students, teachers, and parents about 10 characteristics of the school and its members.
- Teacher Satisfaction Survey (56 items) to report teacher perceptions on nine dimensions of job satisfaction.
- Student Satisfaction Survey (46 items) to collect data on eight dimensions of student satisfaction with school.
- Parent Satisfaction Survey (58 items) to gather parent perceptions on nine dimensions of school operation and services.
- Teacher Report Form (23 items) collects data on teacher perceptions of school/district goals, teacher autonomy, and teacher participation in decision making.
- Student Report Form (8 items) collects student responses on the Brookover Self-Concept of Ability (academic self-concept) scale.
- Principal Questionnaire and Report Form (98 items) to assemble demographic and other pertinent school/district data.

These survey instruments are short and easy to administer; machine-scorable answer sheets are available from NASSP. These instruments provide data on 34 district and school variables, including the six student outcomes above. Conducting the assessment is usually the responsibility of appropriate members of the SIMT. Detailed instructions for entering data and scoring the answer sheets are provided in the CASE-IMS User's Manual which is part of the assessment software package.

Step 5: Interpreting the Data

Translating the data generated by the assessment into a form that can be used for shared decision making is a key step in the process.

The CASE-IMS software includes two related programs. The first program provides data collection and analyses of CASE variables, with the analyses keyed to a bank of some 800 potential intervention strategies. The second program permits simulated alteration of the CASE variables; i.e., a user is able to change the values of all alterable variables (not fixed variables like population) to identify resources or intervention points that would likely improve the effectiveness of a school.

The CASE-IMS program was designed to assist in two important tasks:

1. *Identification of Strengths and Problems:* The program provides easy-to-read graphic displays and printouts of a school's performance on each of the CASE indicator variables. It is possible, for example, to compare the mean scores across different stakeholder groups (i.e., students and teachers, or teachers and parents) on variables such as climate that are common to both groups. The program generates T-scores for users interested in statistical comparisons to show the significance of the differences between means. If a school also collects information about the grade level, sex, or ethnic group of the survey respondents, these

variables may be used to make comparisons within stakeholder groups (e.g., male vs. female teachers).

2. *Planning School Restructuring or Improvement Projects:* School leaders can use the CASE-IMS program to assist with planning for school change in two different ways. First, the system has an "interventions command" to suggest possible actions that a school might take to improve its performance. Second, it provides a "What If" analysis that will predict the effect of demographic trends and/or planned changes on school outcomes. The "What If" analysis uses statistical path equations stored in the CASE data base to estimate potential change in any selected outcomes-variable. For example, what would happen to student satisfaction and student achievement if a school were able to improve the overall school climate score of teachers by an amount equal to the national-norm standard deviation of that variable?

The SIMT is responsible for summarizing and interpreting these data so that they can be used by staff members, student leaders, parents, and others for priority setting and planning.

Step 6: Priority Setting and Planning

Priority setting and planning are processes that ideally should involve the total faculty, other key staff members, parent and community leaders, and student leaders. It is a somewhat lengthy, but important process. The process, which usually functions best in a workshop setting, is designed to accomplish three objectives:

- **Objective #1:** To designate, for each of the variables considered as possible priorities, from three to six interventions perceived by workshop participants to have high potential for positively affecting the variable.
- **Objective #2:** To achieve substantial agreement on which variables should be designated as priorities for school restructuring or improvement for the next one to three years. (Three to six variables are selected.) Positively-rated as well as problem variables should be considered.
- **Objective #3:** To convene school restructuring/improvement task forces to plan and manage activities related to each high-priority variable selected.

These objectives can be accomplished in from six to eight hours of workshop time. The time may be scheduled in several two or three-hour sessions at an in-school or external setting.

Step 7: Task Force Organization and Coordination

Following the priority setting/planning workshop, the SIMT completes two important tasks:
1. Prepares, for each priority variable, a list of school improvement interventions recommended during the workshop.
2. Appoints members to each of the task forces.

Task force *leaders* are either appointed by the SIMT or elected by their membership.

At this point, a short (one or two-hour) training session should be offered to task force members and leaders so that they understand their roles in the implementation process. Additional training for task force members is highly desirable during the year that follows. Training in planning, communications, shared decision making, project management, expediting, managing meetings, and process evaluation can contribute to effective task force operation.

Task forces assume responsibility for planning and implementing activities related to a single significant variable for school restructuring or improvement. They should be viewed as long-term (three years or more) organizational structures.

Step 8: Impact Evaluation and Reassessment

Each year the SIMT should conduct an evaluation of the impact of the restructuring/improvement process on the six CASE-IMS student outcome variables—total achievement, disciplinary referrals, self-efficacy, course success, school year completion, and student satisfaction—and on any other selected outcomes. The same CASE-IMS instruments and procedures used to obtain base-line data (Step 2) can be used again for these evaluations. The results should be reported to central office administrators, the public, the staff, parents, and other interested community leaders.

Schools that effectively implement the eight-step process should be able to report annual improvements in student outcome variables. A complete reassessment and priority setting should take place every three to five years. (The CASE-IMS system is also compatible with the processes required by the regional accrediting associations. More complete information on the system is available in *The CASE-IMS School Improvement Process,* by E. R. Howard and J. W. Keefe, NASSP, Reston, Va., 1991.)

REFERENCES

Archbald, D. A., and Newmann, F. M. *Beyond Standardized Testing: Assessing Authentic Achievement in the Secondary School.* Reston, Va.: NASSP, 1988.

Brandt, R. S., ed. "Restructuring Schools: What's Really Happening." *Educational Leadership,* May 1991.

Carroll, A. W. *Personalizing Education in the Classroom.* Denver, Colo.: Love Publishing, 1975.

Charters, W. W., and Pellegrin, R. J. "Problem Themes." *Educational Administration Quarterly,* Winter 1973.

Chubb, J. E., and Moe, T. E. *Politics, Markets, and America's Schools.* Washington, D.C.: Brookings Institution, 1990.

Coalition of Essential Schools. "The Essential Conversation: Getting It Started, Keeping It Going." *Horace,* 8(2), pp. 1–8.

Coleman, J. S. *Policy Perspectives: Parental Involvement in Education.* Washington, D.C.: U.S. Government Printing Office, 1991.

Dunn, R., and Griggs, S.A. *Learning Styles: Quiet Revolution in American Schools.* Reston, Va.: NASSP, 1988.

Edmonds, R. R., and Frederickson, J. R. *Search for Effective Schools: The Identification and Analysis of City Schools That Are Instructionally Effective for Poor Children.* Cambridge, Mass.: Harvard University Center for Urban Studies, 1979.

Elmore, R. F., and Associates. *Restructuring Schools: The Next Generation of Educational Reform.* San Francisco: Jossey-Bass Publishers, 1990.

English, F. W., and Hill, J. C. *Restructuring: The Principal and Curriculum Change.* Reston, Va.: NASSP, 1990.

Fallows, J. *Japanese Education: What Can It Teach American Schools?* Arlington, Va.: Educational Research Service, 1990.

Frick, T. W. *Restructuring Education Through Technology.* PDK Fastback 326. Bloomington, Ind.: Phi Delta Kappa, 1991.

Fullan, M. G. "Staff Development Innovation and Institutional Development." In *Changing School Culture Through Staff Development,* edited by B. Joyce. Alexandria, Va.: Association for Supervision and Curriculum Development, 1990.

Georgiades, W. *How Good Is Your School.* Reston, Va.: NASSP, 1978.

Georgiades, W.; Keefe, J. W.; Lowery, R. E.; Anderson, W. R.; McLean, A. F.; Milliken, R.; Udinsky, B. F.; and Warner, W. *Take Five: A Methodology for the Humane School.* Los Angeles, Calif.: Parker & Sons, 1979.

Hall, G. E.; Rutherford, W. L.; Hord, S. M.; and Huling, L. L. "Effects of Three Principal Styles on School Improvement." *Educational Leadership* 5(1983).

Hampel, R. *The Last Little Citadel: American High Schools Since 1940.* Boston, Mass.: Houghton Mifflin, 1986.

Hansen, J. H., and Liftin, E. *School Restructuring: A Practitioner's Guide.* Swampscott, Mass.: Watersun Publishing, 1991.

Henderson, A. T.; Marburger, C. L.; and Ooms, T. *Beyond the Bake Sale—An Educator's Guide to Working with Parents.* Columbia, Md.: National Committee for Citizens in Education, 1986.

Hill, J. C. *The New American School: Breaking the Mold.* Lancaster, Pa.: Technomic Publishing, in press.

House, E. R. "Three Perspectives on Innovation." In *Improving Schools: Using What We Know*, edited by R. Lehman and M. Kane. Beverly Hills, Calf.: Sage Publications, 1981.

Howard, E. R., and Keefe, J.W. *The CASE-IMS School Improvement Process.* Reston, Va.: NASSP, 1991.

Huberman, A. M., and Crandall, D. P. *People, Politics, and Practices: Examining the Chain of School Improvement. Vol. IX: Implications for Action.* Andover, Mass.: The Network, 1982.

Hutchins, C. L.; Mayeski, F.; and Salley, M. W., eds. *Achieving Excellence.* Aurora, Colo.: Mid-Continent Regional Educational Laboratory, 1991.

Kaufman, R., and Herman, J. *Strategic Planning in Education: Rethinking, Restructuring, Revitalizing.* Lancaster, Pa.: Technomic Publishing, 1991.

Keefe, J. W. "Personalized Education." In *Organizing for Learning: Toward the 21st Century,* edited by H. J. Walberg and J. J. Lane. Reston, Va.: NASSP, 1989.

———. *Profiling and Utilizing Learning Style.* Reston, Va.: NASSP, 1988.

Keefe, J. W., and Jenkins, J. M., eds. *Instructional Leadership Handbook,* 2d ed. Reston, Va.: NASSP, 1991.

Keefe, J. W., and Kelley, E. A. "Comprehensive Assessment and School Improvement." *NASSP Bulletin,* December 1990, pp. 54–63.

Key, P. L. "Effect of Teacher Roles and Organizational Systems upon Secondary Students' Attitudes Toward Organizational Climate." Doctoral dissertation, University of Southern California, 1977.

Levin, H. M. "About Time for Educational Reform." *Educational Evaluation and Policy Analysis* 2(1984):151–63.

Lewis, A. *Restructuring America's Schools.* Arlington, Va.: American Association of School Administrators, 1989.

Lezotte, L.W.; Hathaway, D. V.; Miller, S. K.; Passalacqua, J.; and Brookover, W. B. *School Learning Climate and Student Achievement.* Tallahassee, Fla.: Florida State University, 1980.

Lieberman, A. *Early Lessons in Restructuring Schools.* New York: National Center for Restructuring Education, Schools, and Teaching. Teachers College, Columbia University, 1991.

Lightfoot, S. L. *The Good High School.* New York: Basic Books, 1983.

Lipsitz, J. *Successful Schools for Young Adolescents.* New Brunswick, N.J.: Transaction, 1984.

Louis, K. S. "Social Values and the Quality of Teacher Work Life." In *Teaching in Secondary Schools,* edited by M. McLaughlin. New York: Teachers College Press, 1990.

Louis, K. S., and Miles, M. B. *Improving the Urban High School: What Works and Why.* New York: Teachers College Press, 1990.

Majkowski, C. *Developing Leaders for Restructuring Schools: New Habits of Mind and Heart.* A Report of the National LEADership Network Study Group on Restructuring Schools. Washington, D.C.: U.S. Government Printing Office, 1991.

McAtee, C. R. "The Effects of the Trump Model and Ten Demographic Variables on Internal Control of High School Students." Doctoral dissertation, University of Southern California, 1977.

McCarthy, R. J. *Initiating Restructuring at the School Site.* PDK Fastback 324. Bloomington, Ind.: Phi Delta Kappa, 1991.

Melaville, A. I., and Blank, M. J. *What It Takes: Structuring Interagency Partnerships To Connect Children and Families with Comprehensive Services.* Washington, D.C.: Education and Human Services Consortium, 1991.

Metz, M. H. "Some Missing Elements in the Reform Movement." *Educational Administration Quarterly,* 24(4), pp. 54–56.

———. "Real School: A Universal Drama Amid Disparate Experience." In *Education Politics for the New Century: The 20th Anniversary Yearbook of Politics of Education Association,* edited by D.E. Mitchell and M.E. Goertz. New York: Falmers Press, 1990.

Michigan Association of Secondary School Principals. *Michigan Schools of the Future Task Force Report: Focus on Restructuring.* Ann Arbor: MASSP, 1990.

Miles, M. B. "Unraveling the Mystery of Institutionalization." *Educational Leadership* 3(1983): 14–19.

Murphy, J., and Evertson, C. *Restructuring Schools: Capturing the Phenomena.* New York: Teachers College Press, 1991.

National Association of Secondary School Principals. *School-Based Management: Theory and Practice.* Reston, Va.: 1991.

———. Task Force on School Environments. *Comprehensive Assessment of School Environments Information Management System (CASE-IMS).* Reston, Va.: NASSP, 1991.

National Association of State Boards of Education. *More Than a Vision: Real Improvements in Urban Education.* Alexandria, Va.: 1990.

National Center on Effective Secondary Schools. "Tracking and Ability Grouping." *Newsletter,* Spring 1990.

———. "Cooperative Learning." *Resource Bulletin,* Spring 1988.

Newmann, F. M. "Student Engagement in Academic Work: Expanding the Perspective on Secondary School Effectiveness." In *Rethinking Effective Schools,* edited by J. Bliss and W. Firestone. New Brunswick, N.J.: Rutgers University Press, in press.

Olson, L. "The Restructuring Puzzle." *Education Week,* November 5, 1988, pp. 7–11.

Powell, A. G.; Farrar, E.; and Cohen, D. K. *The Shopping Mall High School: Winners and Losers in the Educational Marketplace.* Boston: Houghton Mifflin, 1985.

Protheroe, N. J., and Barsdate, K. J. *Culturally Sensitive Instruction and Student Learning.* Arlington, Va.: Educational Research Service, 1991.

Regional Laboratory for Educational Improvement of the Northeast and Islands. *Work in Progress: Restructuring in Ten Maine Schools.* Andover, Mass.: Author, 1991.

Resnick, L. B. *Education and Learning To Think.* Washington, D.C.: National Academy Press, 1987.

Sashkin, M., and Egermeier, J. *School Change Models and Processes: A Review of Research and Practice.* Working draft prepared for the U.S. Department of Education's AMERICA 2000 initiative and for a research symposium to be presented at the 1992 Annual Meeting of the American Educational Research Association. Washington, D.C., 1991.

Scott, A. J. "Evaluating the Cognitive Achievement of LEC Students." Doctoral dissertation, University of Southern California, 1975.

Secretary of Labor's Commission on Achieving Necessary Skills. *SCANS Report.* Washington, D.C.: U.S. Department of Labor, 1991.

Sizer, T. R. *Horace's Compromise: The Dilemma of the American High School.* Boston: Houghton Mifflin, 1984.

Slavin, R. E. "PET and the Pendulum: Faddism in Education and How To Stop It." *Phi Delta Kappan,* June 1989, pp. 752–58.

Spady, W. G., and Marshall, K. J. "Beyond Traditional Outcome-Based Education." *Educational Leadership,* October 1991, pp. 67–72.

Trump, J. L. *A School for Everyone.* Reston, Va.: NASSP, 1977.

Trump, J. L., and Georgiades, W. *How To Change Your School.* Reston, Va.: NASSP, 1978.

Urbanski, A. "'Real Change Is Real Hard': Lessons Learned in Rochester." *Education Week,* October 23, 1991, p. 29.

Villars, J. *Restructuring Through School Redesign.* PDK Fastback 322. Bloomington, Ind.: Phi Delta Kappa, 1991.

Walberg, H. J. "Improving the Productivity of America's Schools." *Educational Leadership,* May 1984, pp. 19–27.

Walcott, H. F. In *Differentiated Staffing,* edited by Scobey and Fiorino. Washington, D.C.: Association for Supervision and Curriculum Development, 1973.

Wehlage, G.; Rutter, R.; and Turnbaugh, A. "A Program for At-Risk High School Students." *Educational Leadership,* March 1987, pp. 70–73.

Weinholtz, D. *Restructuring an Urban School.* PDK Fastback 323. Bloomington, Ind.: Phi Delta Kappa, 1991.

APPENDIX A

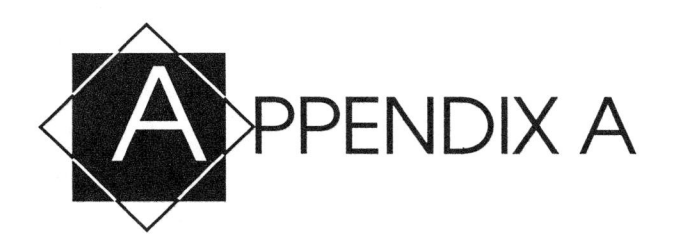

TYPOLOGY OF FACTORS IN SCHOOL IMPROVEMENT

James W. Keefe

These 20 elements are the most significant district and school factors in restructuring.
1. District and State Support: State and district educational agencies provide resources and assistance to restructuring schools. (Re:Learning; Maine)
2. Fiscal Equality: Educational fairness (equity) for all schools, particularly urban settings. (NASBE; ERS)
3. Parental Choice/Involvement: Marketplace model for school choice and/or vital parental involvement in local schools. (Brookings—Chubb and Moe; John Hopkins—Epstein)
4. School-Based Management: Local control of school budget, program, personnel, and decision making. (California, New York, and others)
5. School-Community Agency Coordination: Coordinated counseling and support for families, especially the poor. (NASBE)
6. Shared Decision Making: Participatory decision making vested in the school-site team of administrators and teachers. (NASSP and others)
7. Systematic Change Plan: Step-by-step plan that involves all significant stakeholders (Huberman and Miles; Hall and Hord)
8. Outcome-Based Education: School curriculum and learning environment determined by what students are ultimately expected to do. (Spady)
9. Data-Based Decision Making: School budgeting, planning, and program improvement decisions based on data systematically collected at the local level. (NASSP–CASE; McREL A⁺)
10. Balanced School Climate: Favorable perceptions of the school culture by students, teachers, and parents/community. (Brookover; Lezotte; NASSP–CASE)
11. Teacher Ownership and Engagement: The school environment as a quality workplace and supporter of teacher efforts in program improvement. (National Governors Association; Center on Organization and Restructuring of Schools)
12. Student Engagement in Learning: The school environment provides all students with active learning roles that support student achievement and success. (Learning Environments Consortium; National Center on Effective Secondary Schools)
13. Emphasis on Effort Rather Than Ability: The school environment makes it possible for the weakest students (lowest third) to improve their cognitive skills and to succeed if they try. (Lightfoot; Learning Styles Movement; Japanese Education)
14. Curricular Reduction and Integration: The school program is organized so that students master a limited number of essential skills and areas of knowledge. (Coalition of Essential Schools—Sizer)
15. Provision for Learning in Social Contexts: The school curriculum and instructional program recognizes that learning is embedded in culture and community and that social groups acquire and use information differently. (Resnick; Levin)

16. Emphasis on the Correlates of School Effectiveness:
    - Safe and Orderly Environment
    - Climate of High Expectations for Student Success
    - Instructional Leadership by the Principal
    - Clear and Focused Mission
    - Student Opportunity To Learn and Time on Task
    - Frequent Monitoring of Student Progress
    - Collaborative Home-School Relations
    (Edmonds; Michigan State University; University of Wisconsin-Madison)
17. Optimization of the Essential Factors of School Productivity:
    Student Aptitude
    - Ability or Prior Achievement
    - Development or Maturation

    Instruction
    - Amount of Engaged Learning Time
    - Motivation or Self-Concept

    Environment
    - Supportive Home
    - Classroom Climate
    - Peer Group Influence
    - Reduced Television Viewing
    (Bloom; Bruner; John Carrol; Robert Glaser; Walberg)
18. Implementation of the Elements of Personalized Education
    Diagnosis of Student
    - Developmental Level
    - Learning Style
    - Learning History (Existing Knowledge, Skills, and Attitudes)

    Prescription That Includes
    - Advisement or Mentoring
    - Educational Planning
    - Appropriate Program Placement

    Instructional Flexibility in
    - Teaching Style
    - Instructional Process and Use of Time
    - Study and Thinking Skills Training

    Evaluation of
    - Individual Student Achievement
    - Teacher Performance
    - Program Effectiveness
    (Keefe; Learning Environments Consortium)
19. Research-Based Grouping and Instruction: Student grouping is mixed-age, mixed-grade, and heterogeneous—or at least flexible enough to offset the negative affects of too much stratification; instruction sequences classroom events and employs a variety of options based on research and best practice. (Bloom; Hunter; Rosenshine, Johnson, and Johnson; Slavin; Dunn and Dunn, etc).
20. Authentic Assessment of Student Achievement: New school structures are guided by educational outcomes that 1) produce rather than reproduce knowledge and 2) emphasize disciplined inquiry in:
    - Use of a Prior Knowledge Base
    - In-Depth Understanding Rather Than Superficial Awareness
    - Integration Rather Than Fragmentation of Knowledge. (Newmann; Resnick)

APPENDIX B

OUTCOME-BASED EDUCATION

William G. Spady

Outcome-Based Education (OBE), is founded on three basic premises:
- All students can learn and succeed (but not on the same day in the same way).
- Success breeds success.
- Schools control the conditions of success.

Advocates of Outcome-Based education (OBE) agree that an *outcome* is a successful demonstration of learning that occurs at the culminating point of a set of learning experiences. The term *culminating* refers to the completion point of a segment of curriculum—what students are ultimately able to do at the end, once all formal instruction is over and can be synthesized and applied successfully.

Four Key Principles

Adherents of OBE seek to apply *four key principles* to the design, delivery, documentation, and decision-making work of schooling:

- *Ensure Clarity of Focus on Outcomes of Significance.* Culminating demonstrations become the starting point, focal point, and ultimate goal of curriculum design and instruction. Schools and districts work to carefully align (or match) curriculum, instruction, assessment, and credentialing with the substance (criteria) and processes of the intended demonstration.
- *Design Down from Ultimate Outcomes.* Curriculum and instructional design inherently should carefully proceed backward from the culminating demonstrations (outcomes) on which everything ultimately focuses and rests, thereby ensuring that all components of a successful culminating demonstration are in place.
- *Emphasize High Expectations for All to Succeed.* Outcomes should represent a high level of challenge for students, and all should be expected to accomplish them eventually at high performance levels and be given credit for their performance whenever it occurs.
- *Provide Expanded Opportunity and Support for Learning Success.* Time should be used as a flexible resource rather than a predefined absolute in both instructional design and delivery (to better match differences in student learning rates and aptitudes). Educators should deliberately allow students more than one uniform, routine chance to receive needed instruction and to demonstrate their learning successfully.

What follows is a brief summary of the key approaches that have emerged on the OBE scene to date. The underlying rationale for the framework rests on four key understandings about outcomes and the concept of what it means to be "Outcome-Based."

Four Driving Assumptions

First, outcomes are demonstrations of learning, not the names of subject areas, content, concepts, programs, or themes. Demonstrations can take many forms, but, by definition, they require that whatever learning exists inside the individual be brought to light through some form of observable behavior. These forms can range from filling out answers on a testing sheet to complex demonstrations of role behavior in complex life contexts.

Second, learning demonstrations occur in settings, and *settings* add their own conditions and challenges to the demonstration. Consequently, for an outcome to be "significant"—and matter at a later state in the student's schooling career or life—at least three critical elements that constitute the outcome must all be significant as well:

- The substance being demonstrated;
- The process of the demonstration; and
- The setting in which the process is carried out.

Almost all school outcomes assume that the classroom setting will suffice as a significant demonstration context. Our position is that unless *all three* elements closely resemble the challenges and opportunities students will face in the future, there is no assurance that what is learned in school will have a direct or positive bearing on their life performances following school.

Third, outcomes are *culminating* demonstrations of significant bodies of learning. Culminating means "at the end," when all the previous learning can be synthesized and applied in a best demonstration or performance. It serves as a critical concept in OBE because: (1) OBE's "Design Down" Principle means starting at the culminating point and planning backward from there to the beginning; (2) the culminating point (i.e., ultimate outcome) is, in fact, the focal point for OBE's Clarity of Focus, High Expectations, and Expanded Opportunity Principles; and (3) the culminating outcome is the "bottom line" of instructional delivery, assessment, and student credentialing.

Fourth, *Exit Outcomes* are the ultimate culminating outcomes in a curriculum design and instructional delivery process. From our perspective they pertain to the student as a total human being—not simply to cognitive learning—and represent the totality of the student's learning experiences. This holistic concept means that knowledge, competence, and the student's orientations toward life and success all come into play at the point of exit from schooling. Hence, Exit Outcomes serve as the answer to the ultimate "So what?" question about the purpose and mission of schooling.

THREE BROAD CATEGORIES

Given these four understandings, we believe that the current approaches to defining outcomes and to applying OBE's four principles to their implementation fall into three broad categories: Traditional OBE, Transitional OBE, and Transformational OBE.

- *Traditional OBE* means that *existing curriculum content,* frameworks, and programs are taken as givens and are used to frame and define outcomes. Outcomes are defined from and for the curriculum, rather than the curriculum being "based on" intended outcomes and framed around broader competencies and orientations. Traditional OBE actually engenders a Curriculum-Based Outcomes (CBO) framework and treats content as the fundamental end of the curriculum. If they exist at all in Traditional OBE models, Exit Outcomes are generally about subject matter mastery.
- *Transitional OBE* means that a vehicle exists for separating curriculum content from intended outcomes and for placing primacy on the latter. In this approach, Exit Outcomes clearly exist and are usually defined as broad, often *higher-order competencies and orientations* that cut across or exist independently of specific subject matter content and programs. These broad competencies are almost always content neutral, penetrate down to at least the course level, and often link various kinds of subject matter and concepts together in interdisciplinary curriculum and assessment designs. Content simply becomes a vehicle through which they are developed and demonstrated.
- *Transformational OBE* means that curriculum content is no longer the grounding and defining element of outcomes. Instead, outcomes are seen as *culminating Exit role performances* that include sometimes complex arrays of knowledge, competencies, and orientations and require learning demonstrations in varying role contexts. This makes context (or setting) a very important factor in outcome defining, curriculum design, and assessment, and it dramatically redefines the role of subject content in determining and constraining what outcomes can be. The bottom line of Transformational OBE is that students' learning is manifested through their ability to carry out performance roles in contexts that at least simulate life situations and challenges.

Transformational OBE has its roots in the future-scanning procedures found in well-designed strategic planning and design models. We ask districts to form strategic design teams to thoroughly examine, critique, and synthesize the best available information about the conditions of life students are likely to encounter in their future. These carefully developed descriptions of future conditions serve as the starting point for their OBE design.

Aurora Public Schools in Aurora, Colo., for example, began a serious strategic planning effort in 1990, which resulted in (1) a set of future conditions that drove both their district mission and a set of 28 key learning goals, and (2) a set of five role-based exit outcomes that were derived systematically from the mission and the goals. Both role context and role demonstration elements are evident in their exit outcome framing statement and their outcome statements, two of which are:

We will know we are accomplishing our mission when all our students are:
- Collaborative Workers, who use effective leadership and group skills to develop and manage interpersonal relationships within culturally and organizationally diverse settings.
- Quality Producers, who create intellectual, artistic, practical, and physical products that reflect originality, high standards, and the use of advanced technologies.

Aurora's other statements refer to Self-Directed Learners, Complex Thinkers, and Community Contributors. Work is now underway in Aurora to frame each existing curriculum area around this set of five exit outcomes so that the outcomes serve as the key organizers of all their programs and courses. The district also is developing performance indicators for assessment purposes.

Changes in district program context and structure are sure to follow as the emphasis shifts from completion of traditional subject areas, courses, content, and skills to these higher order, life-role performances. Current programs and courses will facilitate, rather than define, each district's exit outcomes. Strategic decision making, program planning, and resource allocations will all directly reflect the nature and scope of these outcomes.

With its focus on the future, its philosophical commitment to success for all students on Outcomes of Significance in life, and its implications for fundamentally redefining the curriculum, instructional delivery, assessment, and credentialing components of schooling, Transformational OBE gives schools a profoundly different means for restructuring themselves. But it takes vision and a willingness to step beyond the givens of curriculum thinking and program design that have left us mired in an industrial-age model governed by an agricultural-age calendar.

APPENDIX C

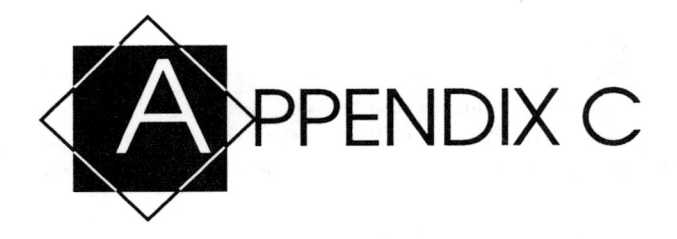

A+CHIEVING EXCELLENCE

MID-CONTINENT REGIONAL EDUCATIONAL LABORATORY

A+chieving Excellence is a site-based decision-making and management system. A+ does not replace an existing program. It is not a new curriculum. It is a system for selecting strategies for improvement and redesign. A+ involves the full staff in setting goals and priorities. It validates what a school is already doing and produces a customized plan for excellence.

A+ uses an original framework for organizing management, curriculum, instruction, and assessment decisions so that limited resources can be directed at strategies and tactics that foster excellence. A+ is an R&D-based information system. Each section is based on recent research and research-based programs. The entire system has been field tested. A+ provides unique tools for assessing school improvement and managing the process of change. It even suggests alternatives to standardized tests. Much of the data can be used to complete mandated "school report cards."

An "expert development process" in A+ reflects the belief that teachers and administrators are professionals with hours of training and the capacity to change—if they have access to a system that harnesses their expertise and secures a commitment to change. A+ focuses on the equalization of achievement between high and low socioeconomic students (who traditionally do less well in school), and 21st century outcomes for all students. (A+ is accepted as a framework for implementing the North Central Association's outcomes-based accreditation process.)

Organization of the System

A+ is organized into an overview and four major sections.
- *Overview* section outlines what A+ is and how to use it.
- *Leadership and Organizational Development* section shows how to manage change. It provides strategies for building a culture that will support change, ways to monitor and predict stages of implementation, and how to set up a site-based decision-making system. Needs assessment tools are included for determining the degree to which the school is currently efficient, effective, and excellent.
- *Efficiency* section determines how the school uses instructional time so as to maximize the amount of time students are engaged in learning.
- *Effectiveness* section explores how the school maximizes the amount of time all students are successful, regardless of socioeconomic status.
- *Excellence* section shows how the school can be redesigned to make sure learning is relevant to the needs of students who will live in the 21st century.

A site-based management council or steering committee composed of the principal, four to six staff members, and someone from the central office guide the school through the process. The full staff, parents, and the community are involved in design sessions to ensure representation of all the school's stakeholders.

Seven Steps to Using A⁺

1. **Develop a decision-making process.**

Establish a site-based management council or steering committee to guide the implementation of A⁺. The council or committee is a representative group of staff members who are responsible for: guiding the implementation of A⁺; gathering the data necessary to determine which parts of, and in which order, A⁺ will be used; planning seminars that will involve the full staff in reviewing A⁺ materials and selecting strategies and tactics for trial implementation; evaluating progress; and developing a long-range plan. The time commitment for a council or committee member is approximately 7 to 10 days spread over about one year.

2. **Collect information about the school's current efficiency, effectiveness, and excellence using needs assessment tools.**

Once the site-based management council or steering committee is selected, it decides whether to collect the data for the three A⁺ units simultaneously or to delay the implementation of the Excellence unit until optimal levels of Efficiency and Effectiveness are reached in the school.

To collect the data, the steering committee can work together or divide into smaller two or three-person teams, each of which focuses on a different data collection task and reports its findings to the committee as a whole. Other staff members can be involved. One such task will be to decide which teachers will collect data in their classrooms.

3. **Analyze the collected data and select a starting point for implementing A⁺.**

This may be a one-time process or a multiple-step activity, depending on whether a school collects data for each A⁺ unit separately or combines the data for two or more units. In either case, the task is to share the data and the council's recommendations for action with the faculty. The A⁺chieving Excellence Survey (AES) can be used to report staff opinions about the areas that are in the greatest need and those that need little improvement.

4. **Select appropriate tactics.**

In addition to collecting and analyzing data about where the school should focus its energy to achieve excellence, an important use of A⁺ is to engage in an inquiry process around the many available options. In effect, A⁺ asks a school to try tactics on an experimental basis, to determine whether they are practical and powerful. Can they be implemented with a minimum of confusion and cost? Do preliminary results suggest the desired improvements?

5. **Set long range goals and develop a plan for A⁺chieving Excellence.**

Once the steering committee has reviewed the data and appropriate sections of A⁺, a draft plan for full implementation of the selected tactics is submitted (if possible) to the participating faculty for consultation and consensus. The plan still represents an inquiry and it will need to be revisited and revised, based on experience.

In addition to specifying the tactics selected from A⁺, the implementation plan includes a consideration of the organizational development that must take place to create a supportive climate for change.

6. **Implement the plan at the organizational and instructional level.**

Implementation must take into account the predictable and slow process by which people deal with change. A reading of the Concerns Based Adoption Model (CBAM) tactic in the Management and Participation section of Leadership and Organizational Development will give a clear understanding of how the implementation process goes through distinct phases and how different kinds of support and information need to be provided at each phase. The implementation plan should be divided into three phases: initial trial and awareness; operational (or mechanical) use; and adaptation and institutionalization.

7. **Adapt and institutionalize the most productive tactics.**

After implementing the initial plan and evaluating the results, a revised plan for A⁺chieving Excellence is developed. This plan focuses on changes that should be made, the rejection of tactics that are not fulfilling strategic goals, the selection of those that give greater promise, and the adoption of plans that best fit the resources, preferences, and unique conditions in the school.

The A⁺ framework below provides a comprehensive view of the system.

A+CHIEVING EXCELLENCE

AN EDUCATIONAL DECISION-MAKING AND MANAGEMENT SYSTEM

LEADERSHIP AND ORGANIZATIONAL DEVELOPMENT

Management and Participation

TACTICS

1. Leadership
2. Collaborative decision making
3. Organizational norms
4. Roles: power and influence
5. Concerns Based Adoption Model (CBAM)
6. Change beliefs
7. Problem sensing and solving
8. Accountability and reporting
- Developing a plan (see Workbook)

Human Development

TACTICS

1. Cultural norms and values
2. Conflict and trust
3. Rewards and incentives
4. Team building
5. Human resource planning
6. Coaching
7. Expert development process

NEEDS ASSESSMENT

TOOLS

1. Academic Efficiency Index (AEI)
2. Achieving Excellence Survey (AES)
3. Success Rate Index (SRI)
4. Disaggregated Analysis
5. Managing School Success Survey (MSSS)
6. Leadstyle

	ABSENTEEISM
Non-Instructional School Activities	
Non-Instructional Class Activities	
Non-Engaged Time (Student inattentiveness)	
Non-Successful Time	
Successful Time	
Relevant Time	

Percentage of Students Enrolled 0% — 100%

Percentage of Time 100% — 0%

EFFICIENCY

SCHOOL MANAGEMENT

TACTICS
1. Reducing dropouts
2. Reducing absences
3. Management approaches to increase efficiency
4. Scheduling approaches to increase efficiency
5. Parental involvement

CLASSROOM MANAGEMENT

TACTICS
1. Beginning the school year
2. Contracting
3. Homework
4. Independent learning
5. Seatwork
6. Student accountability

STUDENT MANAGEMENT

TACTICS
1. Assertive discipline
2. Behavior modification
3. LEAST model of discipline
4. Medick's approach

EFFECTIVENESS

CURRICULUM AND ASSESSMENT

TACTICS
1. College Board's competencies
2. Math proficiency skills
3. Reading proficiency skills
4. Subject matter resources
5. Standardized tests
6. Alternatives to standardized tests
7. Increasing test-taking proficiencies
8. Curriculum alignment
9. Expanding the learning environment
10. Authentic tasks

MOTIVATION AND EXPECTATIONS

TACTICS
1. Releasing student potential
2. Menu of rewards/incentives
3. Motivation survey
4. Praise
5. The multi-ability classroom
6. Alternatives to ability grouping/tracking
7. Student team learning
8. Teacher Expectations and Student Achievement (TESA)
9. Dare to imagine: An Olympian's Technology

INSTRUCTION

TACTICS
1. Active mathematics teaching
2. Beginning Teacher Evaluation Study (BTES)
3. Explicit teaching
4. The 4Mat System
5. Hunter Model
6. Mastery learning
7. Learning to learn
8. Technology
9. Dimensions of Learning
10. Carkhuff's interpersonal skills
11. Cooperative learning

EXCELLENCE

STRATEGIC ANALYSIS

TACTICS

1. External audit (environmental scan)
2. A national scan
3. Implications worksheet
4. Strategic mission
5. Internal audit

RESTRUCTURING

TACTICS

1. Choice
2. Partnerships
3. The Paideia proposal
4. Sizer's Re:Learning
5. Site-based management examples

DESIGN

TACTICS

1. Learning level outcomes
2. Parameters for a 21st century curriculum
3. Backward mapping to the instructional level
4. Backward mapping to the management level
5. The ideal school
6. Examples of design
7. Visions
8. The charette
9. Interagency collaboration
10. Learner-centered guidelines

The A⁺ System Provides a Framework for Site-Based Management, Accreditation, Outcomes-Based Performance, Equitable Outcomes, Redesign, and Restructuring Schools

McREL

2550 South Parker Road • Suite 500 • Aurora, Colorado 80014 • 303-337-0990 • FAX 303-337-3005
4709 Belleview Avenue • Kansas City, Missouri 64112 • 816-756-2401 • FAX 816-753-45657

Appendix D

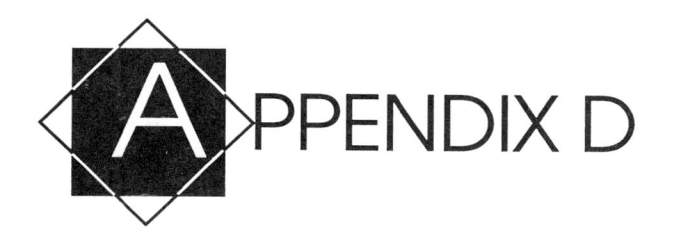

ACTION PLANS FOR NASSP GOAL #1

James W. Keefe
Paul W. Hersey

NASSP will take the lead in "reconceptualizing" and providing models for "restructuring" middle level and high schools for the 1990s, with specific emphasis on new technologies, multicultural sensitivities, international developments, and social issues.

1. Definitional Phase:
   - Solicit information from all states actively engaged in restructuring efforts. (Quick Survey of Principals: Completed: June, 1991)
   - Present a concurrent program with breakout groups at the Orlando NASSP Convention on the topic, "What Are the Key Elements of Restructuring?" The breakout sessions will be conducted as feedback groups and chaired by NASSP Curriculum Committee members who will record participants' views on, "What Are the Key Elements?" (Completed: March, 1991)
   - Data from the state consultations and the Convention breakout groups will go to the NASSP Curriculum Council and representatives of the Curriculum Committee acting as an ad hoc Restructuring Commission. The Commission will synthesize the data and develop a short, preliminary policy statement on "The Key Elements of School Restructuring." (Completed: June and July, 1991)
   - Other standing committees at NASSP concerned with the restructuring definition will be asked for suggestions (i.e., Status and Welfare, Middle Level, Assistant Principals, Urban, Small Schools, Large Schools). Input from other organizations such as the Business Round Table, NGA, etc. will also be sought. (Completed: March-September, 1991)
   - Data relating to restructuring school leadership will be gathered from assessment and development directors operating throughout the United States. Special attention will be given to the skills, knowledges, and abilities leaders must possess to initiate needed educational challenges in schools. (Completed: March-June, 1991)
   - Concurrently, the Executive Director will invite experts on school restructuring to submit short papers describing their models. Authors: Fred M. Newmann, University of Wisconsin-Madison; Theodore R. Sizer, Brown University; William Georgiades, University of Houston, and James W. Keefe, NASSP. (Completed: June-July, 1991)

2. Dissemination Phase
   - A monograph will be developed combining the preliminary policy statement (state and principal data) with the articles by the selected experts. The first chapter will contain the preliminary policy statement, followed by the various models, and then a final chapter with a matrix showing which of the elements are found in the various models. (Draft prepared in September, 1991)
   - The monograph will be circulated to the membership and be subject to widespread consultation during the Fall, 1991 NASSP Regional Meetings, with appropriate recommendations to the NASSP Board of Directors. The Restructuring Commission and NASSP Standing Committees will assist as needed. (Completed: September-October, 1991)

- The process will culminate in a formal policy statement approved and issued by the Board and released at the 1992 NASSP Convention in San Francisco. (February, 1992)
- Other publications dealing with restructuring will be written and distributed to the membership through regular NASSP mailings, conferences and institutes, regional meetings, leadership conferences, etc. (Ongoing)
- A Restructuring "Clearinghouse" of schools successfully meeting a majority of the NASSP standards (key elements) will be initiated by the NASSP Research Department, replacing the existing Exemplary File Directory. (FY 1993)
- As funds become available, visits will be arranged to schools modeling some or all of the key elements of restructuring contained in the NASSP definition. As these site reviews are completed, a list of prototypes demonstrating systemwide changes in secondary schooling will be developed. (FY 1993)
- NASSP will work closely with the state associations to encourage task forces and other support for district and school restructuring efforts. (Ongoing)

3. Development Phase

Following the definition and dissemination phases, a development strategy will be initiated. (1992–1997)

- Long term "practitioner based" development programs such as Springfield, Leader 123, From the Desk of . . ., Mentoring and Coaching, Let's Talk—How Leaders Communicate, Motivation, and University Alliance efforts will be offered through state assessment and development offices, state departments of education, universities, LEAD centers, etc. The emphasis in these programs will be on giving school leaders the unique skills and abilities to lead the restructuring movement. Follow-up processes and techniques will be emphasized. (Ongoing)
- A major focus of the National Institute Programs will be school restructuring concepts. A number of national demonstration programs will be offered to vertical teams of administrators and teachers as well as to individual principals and assistant principals and other administrators. Understanding the restructuring concepts (knowledge base) and their implementation will be a paramount consideration in the design of these programs. (FY 1993 and beyond)
- Special programs on restructuring for unique segments of the NASSP membership will be initiated (e.g., assistant principals and middle level principals). The focus will be on practical approaches to initiating restructuring in schools. (FY 1993)
- Restructuring programs to meet the unique needs of urban, suburban, and rural school principals and assistant principals will be developed. Special attention will be given to appropriate training of staff members working with culturally diverse students. (FY 1993 and beyond)
- Audiovisual aids, workbooks, and special materials will be developed to assist members with restructuring efforts. A special emphasis on services to isolated members who generally do not attend conferences or other formal NASSP programs will be a part of this effort. (FY 1993 and beyond)
- NASSP will collaborate with one local school district to establish an America 2000 experimental school or apply for funding of a prototype "New American School." (1992 and beyond)
- A program to recruit minorities into education and administration through personal and professional mentoring support will be initiated. Restructuring educational leadership will necessarily include the recruitment and inclusion of more minorities on the school leadership team. (FY 1993 and beyond)
- Principal leadership strategies for initiating partnership programs in schools will be developed involving Local School Councils (LSC), business and industry, community organizations, and parents. (Ongoing)
- A new "Initiative" development module will be offered to school leadership teams. A developmental emphasis will be placed on such skills as risk taking, teaming, collaborative decision making, planning, implementation, developing, measuring, forecasting, delegating, etc. (FY 1992 and beyond)
- Technical assistance in restructuring strategies will be provided to the membership through the Professional Assistance office. (FY 1993 and beyond)
- A special theme (Restructuring Schools) will be planned for the 1993 NASSP National Convention. A series of programs, clinics, demonstration, and curriculum activities will be provided for Convention attendees. (FY 1992)